LIVIN
THE L...

A Northern Irish Memoir

by

Arthur Magennis

Beaten Track

www.beatentrackpublishing.com

Beaten Track

First published 2014 by Beaten Track Publishing
Copyright © 2014 Arthur Magennis

A CIP catalogue record for this book
is available from the British Library.

ISBN: 978 1 909192 77 5

Beaten Track Publishing,
Burscough. Lancashire.
www.beatentrackpublishing.com

Thanks to my genius daughter, Nuala, for typing, editing and getting this book into chronological order, and my wife, Noreen, for putting up with months of scribbling.

Arthur's parents wedding in 1918
Left to right:
Back Row: Patrick McKeever, Teresa Magennis (bride), James Magennis (groom) Maggie McGeown, Hugh Canavan.
Front Row: John McGeown, Alice Mallon, Tommy Canavan, John Mallon, Minnie Canavan.

Across the moss dead silence reigns
A turf man drowses in the heat
His dog with one eye open sleep does feign
And quietly his watch will keep.
The man's head gradually hangs lower
Until his chin rests on his chest
And faraway across the heather
A curlew calls its young ones to their nest.
A lark then suddenly breaks cover
Singing and climbing to the sky
The dog is interested just enough
To open up a bit his other eye.
The man now stares and looks around
Awakened by his own intrusive snore
Looks at the sun and at his turf
Then settles down to sleep once more.
But on another bank, What's that?
A hare, blissfully unaware,
Is hopping gracefully along,
Happy and without a care.
Downwind the dog picks up the scent
And howling leaps up from his lair
Disturbing the geese in a nearby swamp
Which shrilly squawking fill the air
And the turf man stands alone in shock
His siesta ruined now beyond repair.

CHAPTER ONE

When Eileen Hughes stepped into our farmhouse kitchen my mother greeted her with a smile. Eileen stood there in a knee length swagger mohair coat with a fur collar, and she may even have had a hat with a small veil.

She was a tall, handsome woman with striking dark blue eyes, and had arrived for the evening in order to relate her adventures of the previous night when she had gone to a dinner party in a Dungannon hotel.

My mother loved these get-togethers, I think because she had come from a more upmarket background herself but, now, as a farmer's wife with a family to tend to, she had to be content with secondhand dining out.

Eileen lived in the next farmhouse to us, about 200 yards away, with her mother and father, Kate and Peter, and her brother, Jim Joe. It was a home from home for us kids, and Peter, who had returned from America where he had worked in the carriage trade with horses, used to tell me stories about it.

"Holy boots," he would say – that was his only swear word. "To watch the lights along the Hudson River was a magnificent sight."

We lived in Derryvarn, which is a subdivision of the townland of Derrytresk in County Tyrone, Northern Ireland. Derryvarn consisted of ten long thatched farmhouses built along the main road to Coalisland with their gable ends towards the road and nearly all facing east, as were most houses at that time.

There were but two cars in our locality then – the teacher's and the priest's – and we all travelled by bicycle. Everyone had a bike, which had the same status as a horse in western films, where horse stealing was a hanging offence. The bike could be left anywhere and it wouldn't be touched.

In the town, of course, the doctor and the businessmen had cars and the newly qualified blond son of the chemist would deliver prescriptions in a red sports car speeding over our bumpy roads.

Eileen, who was a children's nurse, worked for a rich Protestant family in Lurgan and later Upperlands, Co. Derry, where she was highly thought of as she was a very capable woman. As the only way to live the life she wished, Eileen had to pick only boyfriends who were mobile, and so it was that a succession of men, all on four wheels, would whisk Eileen away to another evening in the town. Sometimes on the way she would call at our general store for her cigarettes and depart in a cloud of perfume. To give her her due, she was no snob and a lorry or a van would suffice at times.

The following day she would call round to see Teresa, my mother, and, when the tea and cake were served and we kids had taken up our viewing positions around the kitchen, she would give a blow by blow account of the evening in detail from the starter to coffee and interspersed with many sherries, of which she seemed to be quite fond.

Sometimes we missed important bits, as the voices would drop quite low, but we knew we weren't supposed to hear these.

In the summer evenings these sessions could last until midnight, which did not please my father, at all. Tomorrow the cows would be waiting to be milked and we had to be fed and sent to school and, Eileen, as she was on holiday from her nursing career, could sleep all day if she wished. My father didn't think it quite fair.

Arthur's mother, Teresa, with Eileen Hughes

One night, of course we were all in bed, she left about 11:30 p.m. and, as usual, they continued the conversation as my mother would walk her to the corner, where Eileen turned right to go home. Time passed and my father was getting restless as it was past their bedtime and he had done his rounds and locked up. Suddenly the clock struck midnight and he walked out to the gate and looked up to the corner, and there they stood in the moonlight, still engrossed. What did he do? He stood on the road, flapped his arms and crew like a cock. It didn't have the desired effect as the two of them panicked and came running back again. In the end my father had to escort Eileen right to her door.

I was born in 1926 and had three older sisters, Mary, Kathleen and Elizabeth, and a younger brother and sister, Shamey and Peggy; Mary, the eldest, sadly died of TB at the age of twenty-two.

There were two farms belonging to the Magennis family. My father, James, was born on farm one and he had two brothers, Joe and Peter. Peter, the eldest, inherited farm one when my grandfather, Arthur, died, and Joe inherited farm two. My father, the youngest, went to Edinburgh to work in the liquor trade.

Joe, who had also a pub/grocery business at number two farm, set about building a large two storey barn of stone and slate. It was a big undertaking at the time and he got into debt, so much so that my father had to come home to rescue him, which makes me think he would have been more than a barman to be able to do this. He bought the farm from Joe but still owed him a balance.

Joe then emigrated to America with his family and recently his son, Joe, came over to see us but has since died. When we were young long letters would arrive from America and we had to be quiet while Daddy read Joe's letter. The same thing would happen while he replied; dead silence was observed while he wrote to Uncle Joe. They seemed to be very close friends. My sister, Kathleen, who is four years older than I, says that she always saw him putting money in the letter.

The big two storey barn and loft were eventually completed and it looked as if we were permanent citizens of Derrytresk farm number two.

Arthur, 16, in front of two-storey barn

The land around where we lived flooded in winter time as nearby Lough Neagh couldn't take the extra rain. Our house was on a hillside overlooking fields and meadows about half a mile from the Blackwater River which meandered around us from south to north, until it reached Lough Neagh a few miles further on.

When I was born, Northern Ireland had just been created – invented might be a better word. Britain had decided to withdraw from Ireland, but the Unionists of Northern Ireland objected to it and their wishes were granted, in spite of the democratic principle that the wishes of the majority are paramount. The Unionists were a minority in the nine counties of Ulster, so six of the nine counties were cordoned off with an imaginary border and the province of Northern Ireland was born.

The reason for the concentration of Protestant Unionists in the northern corner of Ireland goes back to 1611 and the plantation of Ulster. After the defeat of the Irish by a massive army sent over by Queen Elizabeth I, the British advertised for settlers to come and fill the places left by the Irish, who had either been killed or driven into the bogs. These were called the planters and they came in their thousands, the majority being Scottish Presbyterians who were not a good choice for peaceful coexistence, as they hated Catholics to such an extent that they wouldn't celebrate Christmas, because they thought it was a Catholic festival; it wasn't until 1950 that they were allowed to do so. They celebrated the New Year instead. The New Year is the feast of the circumcision of Jesus, which is an important day in the Jewish calendar and it became a Christian holiday as well. That is why New Year is celebrated.

In 1926 I was born into a bigoted society where it was arranged that Catholics could never have a majority. The recent Good Friday agreement has changed all that and Northern Irish people have equal rights, irrespective of their colour or creed now, and they are managing to live together in comparative peacefulness.

Of course, when the 'planters' arrived they only wanted the best land and when they reached the Blackwater River from the north, they would have stopped and looked across at Derrytresk and, if it was winter, seen only floods, half a mile wide along the river bank and reaching as far as they could see north and south, and in the background the hill of Derryvarn and Derrytresk surrounded by bog land. They were not going to risk their lives crossing the river for floods and swamps.

So Derryvarn and its situation adjacent to the river, separating it from the settlers, became a microcosm of the Plantation of Ulster.

I suppose after a time the Irish, who had escaped the massacre, came out of the bogs and settled in the unclaimed land which flooded in the winter but where the meadows, called the Brilla, could be grazed in the summer months. At that time, my ancestors may have been amongst them. I don't know if any records were kept or saved from that time. My father was born in 1872 and died in 1954, and my grandfather, Arthur, could have been born in the mid 1800s.

Most of the Irish who were driven off their land settled in the bogs. They built houses from timber and zinc, which wouldn't sink in the bogs but were freezing cold in the winter time. Many got jobs working for the peat company.

The river could not be seen from our door, as the bank was much higher than the surrounding land. When I was very young I remember being held up at the front door to see the floods which came right up to the foot of the hill below our house. The Brilla and fields looked like one large lake. In later years Lough Neagh was lowered in drainage schemes and the Brilla became beautiful meadows all year round.

A steamer came up the river at eleven o'clock each morning. All that we could see from our house was the top of its red and black funnel as it belched its black smoke into the air. It came across the lough from Belfast about thirty or forty miles away and it towed a long chain of lighters or barges laden with coal and Indian corn. Just about opposite our house it would blow its loud horn for two or three minutes and soon we would see the hauliers trotting past on their way to pick up the lighters and tow them up the canal to Coalisland, where the big dray horses would distribute the cargo around the coal yards and mills.

When we were in the meadows, the steamer was a sight to behold, especially when we were young. We'd wait on the bank expectantly until we heard it in the distance and then it would come past with a vengeance, smoke belching, engine pounding, and just as quickly it would disappear round the bend. In contrast, the lighters would suddenly appear, moving absolutely without a sound. We would start to count them – one, two, three – and usually there would be about eight or nine, all strung out along the river, with someone at the tillers guiding them around the bends and away from the banks.

The steamer and the lighters would go on a few more miles to a place called 'The Point' where the Coalisland canal joined the Blackwater River and the hauliers would collect the lighters and tow them to Coalisland along the towpath and through the locks.

That was very relaxing to see on a nice day, as the horse would plod silently along the towpath while the great lighter would move silently behind. Some people went down to the locks in the good weather just to see it.

Some of our farm helpers would know a few of the barge men because, as they lived on the barges and could be a day or two in the area while they unloaded, they would come up to our shop for supplies.

"Hello Atty," one would call to a man who always had a black and white fox terrier sitting on the prow looking very important, and they would exchange a few words. His name was Atty Mullen.

Our shop was situated on the corner of the crossroads and our farmhouse was about 100 yards further down the road. It was known in the area as Magennis' Corner and was a meeting place for people. The main road sometimes was busy with big lorries which carried large loads of peat away to the towns. On dole days, the road would be busy with bicycles as the men went to sign on on Tuesdays and collect their money on Fridays. On Saturday mornings, the road would be busy again, with horse, pony and donkey carts, laden with peat turf for customers in Coalisland and Dungannon. This was the day that I would wait at the corner with my penny to ask someone to get me a pennyworth of marbles. I was always very excited, waiting to get the bag and open it, as there were so many beautiful colours. But, if I had a favourite, I was sure to lose it at school the next week.

Our house was the typical long thatched farm house of the time. All the houses in Derryvarn were the same, but ours had been modernised a bit, although the fireplace still had the black iron crook that had a hinge at the side and swung out and back again with the boiling pot or kettle so that it could be lifted off from the fire.

There was a big crook and a little crook – the little one for the kettle and the other one for the pots, small medium and very large, which I think my mother and Frances, who was our maid of all work, boiled clothes in.

Frances, who lived a few hundred yards from us, had a more primitive earlier fireplace called a backstone fireplace. In this you could walk right under the chimney breast and look up into the sky through a big wide space. I imagine a lad could have abseiled down it. Instead of a ceiling, a large platform came out from the fireplace and reached a quarter of the way across the kitchen. This was called the farry and on it you threw everything that you wished to keep dry, including the horse's collar.

By the side of this fire, right under the chimney, the jinny lamp was hung on a nail in the wall. This was a tin about half a pint in size with a spout like a teapot. It was filled with paraffin, the wick

12

protruding from the spout, and when it was lit at dusk it gave a long streaky, smoky flame, which, of course, went straight up the chimney. The jinny would be lit long before the main oil lamp.

Some of the houses still had earthen floors that felt cold on our bare feet when we went in. In later years they would all be concreted over.

We also had a ceiling in the roof, which was unusual, as in most of the houses when you looked up you saw the scraws – fibrous sods cut from the bogs – and the great black oak purlins bearing the roof.

The top end of our house was where we originally had a pub and our wide cindered forecourt, which we called a street, had a double gated entrance so that horse drawn vehicles could drive in and park or turn. I think it was in the early 1920s that the licensing laws were changed, because of the proliferation of pubs, perhaps, and our pub was closed. The only pub in the area then, belonging to Mr. Falls, was about a mile away. I remember my mother was very pleased with this, she said, because she hated the fights that broke out in the street at the weekends. Maybe the liquor was too potent.

When I was small I used to play with a lot of pewter whiskey measures, ranging from the smallest – not much larger than a thimble – to about a pint size. They had a blueish tint and were very ornate. I loved lining them all up in order of size. I suppose there were about a dozen altogether.

My father was in his fifties when I was born and also lame from an accident he'd had a few years earlier, when a loaded cartwheel ran over his leg and smashed it. He had a steel plate down the front of his leg, which fascinated us when we were young and we used to count the studs screwed into it. He always had to use a stick to walk afterwards.

On the morning that my sister Kathleen was born, my father had just got out of hospital and was on two sticks. It was 4th May, 1922. The Black and Tans were proceeding with an operation which became known as the Round Up. They rounded up every able-bodied man in the district and marched them three or four miles into Clanoe, where they herded them into a field. When the officer in charge saw my father hobbling in, he said, "What did you bring him for?" and told him to go home again.

I wrote a little poem on Kathleen's ninetieth birthday card. She may have been only a few hours old but she was there.

On the morning of the 4th May,
90 years ago today,
The Black and Tans came to the door
and took your dad away.
They rounded up every man
from the river to Ardbo
And marched them all three miles or more
to a field beside Clanoe
'Who brought this man?' the Captain said,
'A sorry sight indeed.
Go home again, the way you came,
your sort we do not need.'
So back he went upon his sticks,
as fast as he was able,
Which wasn't very fast, at all,
to see his wife and baby.

14

The Black and Tans had arrived in Ireland in March, 1920. A year earlier the British government had advertised for men for a "rough and dangerous task". Former British Army soldiers had come back home from the Great War to unemployment and happily joined the Black and Tans for ten shillings a day. There weren't enough uniforms to go round and they wore khaki jackets and Royal Irish Constabulary dark trousers, hence the name.

They set about a programme of terrorism and their atrocities were legendary, so my father would have known not to protest or he would have been shot.

As in England, the upper classes were in agreement about one thing: keep the lower classes uneducated, unable to read and write, otherwise they will be able to see through the myth that they are inferior beings. The cut glass accent was part of this and people respected it as a voice of authority that could be trusted. Not anymore, though. At the time of the troubles in Northern Ireland the press boys coined the phrase, "Please leave your message after the high moral tone," which they said was recorded on the answering machines in London.

My father hadn't much education, apart from reading and writing, but he went to night school later on. When we brought home mathematical problems from school, he would do them in his head, but he couldn't tell us how it was done.

He was easy-going and a figure of authority in the background. If the girls wanted to go to dances when they were young, they would go to Daddy first and he would promise to do his best for them, as my mother was very strict.

I never knew my father as a young man who could kick a ball around with his son, although his contemporaries would often tell me that, in his younger days, he could run like a hare. And one woman called Nellie, to whom I used to deliver flour, would smile at me and say, "Oh, you're like your dad. Your dad was a bit of lad."

He looked after the shop all day, every day, and had a man to do the farm work, giving him instructions each morning. Alongside the usual groceries, he supplied the local farmers with cattle, horse and pig feed, as well as sacks of flour as everyone made soda bread. It was delicious and I can still taste it.

He stocked animal medicines and ointments and advised the farmers what to use. He also stocked farming implements, like spades, forks and anything a farmer needed: medicine, knitting wool, paraffin, treacle, salted herrings. These are some of the things I remember. Of course, cigarettes and tobacco were the biggest sellers as everyone smoked. And the sales continued even after the shop closed, for people came down to the house for cigarettes almost until bedtime.

When we were sitting around the fireside at night and a knock came to the door, whoever happened to be nearest would go out into the dark hall and open the door. We could never see who it was, but we could usually guess from the voice and call them by name. It was always cigarettes. "Give us ten Players, Arthur," a voice would say. I'd go in, get the Players, take the money, drop it into a silver gravy boat that sat on the sideboard and resume my seat. If my father went to the door he would say the same to everyone – "Hello, Juh" – that way he covered fifty percent of the names.

On Saturday, Charlie, our farm man, would deliver loads of animal feed around the country. I went with him, of course, and I got to know about every house and its occupier in the area.

When the cart stopped I'd jump off and run into the house or run around the yard while Charlie and the owner would be unloading. I loved those trips in the summer but in the winter, if I was foolish enough to go with Charlie, I would regret it. Sometimes coming home late on a frosty evening, really cold, the houses would all be lit up and through the windows I could see people getting the evening tea ready, exuding warmth and reminding me that I was freezing and starving. The last mile or so seemed to last forever.

When we came home about six o'clock the kitchen would be bright and warm and the tea would be on the table. The radio would be playing and next we would hear the introduction for *Dick Barton, Special Agent* and I would sit spellbound, while Dick, Jock and Snowy knocked the daylights out of the baddies.

Sometimes, when I got home after visiting all those houses in the surrounding area with Charlie, my mother would ask me what a house was like.

"It was all right," I would say.

"What kind of kitchen did they have?"

"It was all right," I would reiterate.

"Didn't you notice anything at all?" she would say. "You're not much good to send out anywhere."

Now I realise how frustrating it must have been, as my mother was very furniture and fashion conscious.

There was a black and white wall with a smooth surface that ran along the road opposite the shop, and on Sunday mornings after Mass, if the weather was good, people would gather and sit on the wall. When it was full they sat along the hedge. I suppose they were just there for somewhere to go or, maybe, for the craic. Craic is a Gaelic word meaning fun which we added to our English vocabulary, because there doesn't seem to be an English word with the same meaning. Everybody loved a bit of craic. If you complained about someone to my mother she would say, "Ah, but isn't he great craic," and that was that. I think it was a form of repartee which is the nearest I can get, but it had to be witty – everyone likes a laugh.

On Sunday evenings another crowd would gather at the corner to play pitch and toss, because the Irish do like a gamble. It would start about seven o'clock and the crowd would get bigger and bigger, surrounding the wide sandy space on the quiet road opposite the shop. One night, my father was late locking up because the trade in cigarettes and minerals and the like was good and he said, when he came home, that there were perhaps thirty men there in the circle, and they were striking matches to see if the coins were heads or tails.

Gambling on horse and dog racing was also a great craze. My father had the weekly handicap books stacked behind the door in his bedroom. These were cross reference books and he could look up any horse and find out its history and past form at any time. When my father was ill and had to get Dr. Girvan from Coalisland, who also would have had a flutter, the doctor drew back the bedclothes and there underneath was the handicap book.

"Ah, James," he said. "I see, like myself, you study the bible."

It's raining today and it hasn't stopped
since I had my breakfast call
I kneel with my head against the pane
and watch the raindrops fall
For a while I settle in a trance
but I want to go out and play
Oh, I wish it would stop, I wish it would stop
for today is Saturday.
I wanted to go with Jimmy and Joe
down to the water edge
We could skim some stones and hide in the den
we made behind the hedge
Afterwards, if the sun is warm,
we could go down for a swim
This time I promise I won't be scared,
I'm going to jump right in.
Mum, the rain has stopped and it's getting bright
and the sun's coming out again
Well, off you go but come straight back
if you feel one drop of rain
And off I go three hops and a jump, three hops and a
jump, warm in the morning sun
I'll be there soon, I'll be there soon,
and I break into a run
Oh what a day it's going to be,
a Saturday of fun.

CHAPTER TWO

I didn't like school right from the first day. Kathleen took me by the hand and told me about another little boy who was starting school that day as well, and what a nice little boy he was, as we walked along. I suppose I was probably crying. I remember we got to the door and when I heard the harmonium playing I bolted and ran all the way home.

School Photo from around 1931
Arthur is 6th from left on front row (no shoes).
Also, on the school photo is 'The Mistress', standing left,
Kathleen, 9, back row, 2nd from left, Mary, 11, middle row, 6th
from left, and Elizabeth, 7, middle row 7th from left.

After that I had to be watched, as I would bolt at the first opportunity. The big boys would be sent to catch me, as well as people in houses along the way. But it seemed I kicked anyone in my way on the shins and I always got home.

Recently, Shamey was talking to a man called Joe Mor who was in Dungannon hospital with a bad heart and he asked him, "How is Arthur?"

Shamey replied, "He's all right."

"Well, tell him I've still got a black bump on my shin where he kicked me."

I must have settled down eventually. In the wintertime at school we were given a mug of cocoa about eleven o'clock each morning from a big enamel bucket in the playground. School was heated by two coal fires; one in the upper infants' room and the other in the bigger senior room. The large room was always cold.

The cane was used a lot and was something one had to get used to. It was part of school at that time and I think it was very cruel when one considers the tiny hands and the cruelty that seemed to be part of the adult culture of the time.

Our school had a headmaster called the Master and a headmistress known as the Mistress, and an assistant teacher who taught the infants up to first grade. The Master had a weakness which was called 'the drink' and was a common affliction in Ireland. The Master was a binge drinker, which meant he could go sober for a long time and then suddenly break out and go on the tear, as we called it.

When he showed signs of erupting, the Mistress and her family usually took precautions and watched him closely. Alcoholics can be very clever, devious and extremely difficult to watch. At this particular time they got a friend and neighbour of the Master's, called Tommy, to sleep in his room with him when they first saw the signs that he had been at the bottle. Knowing he would stop at nothing to get out, they had his clothes removed lest he escaped during the night.

One night, Tommy woke up to find that the Master had disappeared. He rushed to put his clothes on but they were gone as well. The Master was small and squarely built, and Tommy was very long and skinny, so the idea of him being seen in public in his new outfit would have given the Mistress palpitations. Respectability and keeping up appearances were most important.

Members of the family went in different directions and during the afternoon he was located in a pub rendering all of his favourite songs and entertaining the customers, still dressed in his special clothes.

We dreaded him returning to school because he would be in a terrible temper when he was coming off the drink. One morning he came in early and lined us all up to examine our readers. We had to stand in front of him and hold up our reading books as he laid the cane against the page and peered at it to see if the corners of the pages were turned up. Dog's ears, he called it. Nearly everyone was severely caned that morning – I think I can still feel it.

In spite of the cane there was plenty of fun at school. One day in the reading class a little girl called Mary Ellen couldn't say 'the' – she would say 'de', instead. The teacher said to her that to say 'the' she should put her tongue out, showing her how to do it. So Mary Ellen said 'de' then stuck out her tongue afterwards. Of course, we all laughed and giggled in spite of a fear of the cane.

Another girl called Molly, who was very scared of the cane, wouldn't hold out her hand for the punishment, or she would hold it out and then pull it away at the last second. She was really terrified. The Mistress told her that she would give her another blow if she pulled her hand away again. So Molly got hold of her left wrist with her right hand in order to keep her hand there but, when the Mistress came down with the cane, Molly jumped back out of the way. The Mistress made another swipe and she jumped back again and off they went around the class room. In spite of the fear in us we all started laughing again. It was very funny to watch.

One day the inspector came and asked some of our class to read aloud poems he selected from our reading books. One girl was asked to read a poem which started, "The Assyrian came down like a wolf on the fold And his cohorts were gleaming in purple and gold."

She read out in a very high confident voice, "And his corsets were gleaming in purple and gold."

When we all roared with laughter she just stared at us as she didn't realise what she had said.

The inspector smiled a little then said, "Very good, very good. Now, next please."

After school, our family of six children normally made our way to Hughes' where we were always welcomed by Peter.

"Holy boots," he would say, "But you're getting bigger every day." And he would sometimes produce a Victorian penny stained with tobacco, as most of the pennies at that time were, or a sweet. We just walked in, sat down and, as kids do, missed nothing.

Peter and Jim Joe ran the farm but the main thing about Hughes' was that it was open house to everyone. Tramps and anyone down on their luck came and went at will. Peter would look after them and feed them, and they would sleep in the barn or somewhere around the house.

Mrs. Hughes had her own special tramps with names like Bright Maria, Strabane Annie and Kate Shaw. Mrs. Kate Hughes was a fat woman and she and Peter were not as young as they had been, although Peter was a very fit upright man for his age. The first thing that fascinated me was his gold tooth, which shone like a beacon and made a clicking sound when he chewed. I never tired of watching it.

Mrs. Hughes sat on her especially wide chair in the corner next to the hearth with her snuff box sitting on her stomach. She would share her snuff with Bright Maria when she dropped in for a day or two. Bright Maria had two little sparkling eyes like a bird and perhaps that's where she got her nickname.

Kate Shaw, a plump lady in her fifties, had long conversations with Mrs. Hughes and they were punctuated by Kate's favourite expression.

"Well blessed to God and deed by jint," she would say when she wanted to emphasise her latest tale, of which she had many. Mrs. Hughes sat listening and nodding but she seemed to enjoy it all.

Peter was on best terms with all the dogs in the area for he carried pieces of bread and titbits for them. You would see him take something from his pocket and give it to them and they would follow him everywhere.

He was a keen gardener, growing all his own vegetables, and he surrounded the house with flowers and plants and little arbours overgrown with rambling roses. He would plant rambling roses along the roads as well, and the hedges on the road past our house would be beautiful in the summer. Altogether Peter was a saintly man.

Jim Joe, on the other hand, was a different person. A handy man with brains who could do most anything with building and machinery, but his moods were unpredictable and, over the years, caused many disagreements between himself and Peter.

For ploughing in the spring and harvesting in the autumn, neighbouring farmers would join together. A plough and mowing machine required two horses to pull them, but each farm had only one horse each. This system saved people having to keep two horses just for the spring and autumn. Naturally we joined with the Hughes'. My father supplied the machine and the horse, Jim Joe supplied his mare and himself, as he did the ploughing, in which he took great pride. If his furrow wasn't dead straight he wouldn't be happy. Later, when he allowed me to have a go, he described my furrow as "like a dog piddling in snow" and woe to you if you let the outside horse come around too quickly on the turn and injure the inside horse.

But in those early years of my childhood I would come home from school and see Jim Joe and the horses in the field, surrounded by a cloud of seagulls having a feast of fat worms. I would run along in the furrow behind him and the cool clay felt beautiful on my bare feet.

In the wintertime we children wore heavy nail boots, like the farmers and the farm labourers, as our roads were surfaced with loose cut stones and were hard on shoes. In the summer, most of the boys would go barefoot which is something we looked forward to, our feet becoming very tough so that we could even run over the stony roads. My mother tried to make us wear sandals, which the girls did, but I would take mine off and shove them under the hedge. One could not be different from the majority. As we didn't use the roads much anyway and had a short cut through the moss, bare feet was an ideal and pleasant way to travel as the moss was soft and cool on the feet and was also very clean.

The down side to being reared on a farm was that as you got older you had jobs to do, such as setting potatoes. When the fields were ploughed and harrowed and the drills were opened, dead straight of course by Jim Joe, then seed potatoes would be brought out to the headland and we would each don a sack apron tied around our waist, lift the bottom up and fill it with potatoes, and proceed with the backbreaking task of planting along each drill – one potato for each step. Of course, to children that was monotonous but it had to be done and it was more readily tolerated because we were allowed to stay off school.

There was a lot of work to do, what with the shop and the farm, so we always had a man of all work who could turn his hand to anything. The first one I remember was Pat Connolly. He had a tattoo of an anchor on his wrist which was fascinating to me. He seemed to stay on after work and ceilidh, as it is called, and sometimes my mother would ask him to sing, as he had a nice voice and he always sang the same song: "When the fields are white with daisies, I'll return".

He had a very good voice and all the Connollys were musical. I must have been very small because I can remember one night, my mother got me ready for bed and then she said, "Now you must go to the toilet or you might w-e-t the bed," spelling it out. That was a habit she had with Frances when they were speaking, because little ears pick up everything and repeat what has been said at embarrassing times.

"No, you mustn't wet the bed," said Pat.

"Mammy," I whispered, as she was carrying me out, "I think Pat knows the meaning of w-e-t the bed."

Another time, when I was having rice pudding with golden syrup on it, which was a great favourite of the family as a special treat, I couldn't finish it, as it was very filling, but I had seen my sister Mary putting hers on a high shelf in a cupboard and I said, "Mammy, I'm going to hide my p-i-g rice." I suppose I thought no one would know what I meant and I was very cunning, indeed.

Pat went away to work in England and when he came back home again, he said Hitler was getting belligerent. This was about 1935 and he thought there was going to be a war, but it was another few years before the war started.

I was bigger then and I remember he called in to see us one Sunday when he came home. He was wearing a stone coloured mac and when my mother remarked how nice it was, he said, "That, Mrs. Magennis, is what's called a swallow mac and it's lined with teddy bear fur," and he opened it and displayed the furry lining.

Pat's successor was James, or Ned's James, as he was known. James whistled and sang his way through life. He was quite young and I followed him around the farm. I suppose I was about eight or nine at the time. James sang and I sang with him and then he told me that I wasn't swinging it enough. At that time, everyone was going to the pictures, black and white, of course – Charlie Chaplin and Gracie Fields were the stars – but not us children, of course. It would be years before I would go, but James knew all the latest songs and how to swing it. So then the two of us would be swinging it in the middle of the potato field, hands swinging and body swaying, until he was satisfied that I had got it right.

Then he taught me to stand on my head. We were in the middle of a field one day and I think James was mowing rushes, when he decided to stand on his head. Of course, I tried to do the same but just fell over, so he got my feet and told me to grip the grass with my hands making a triangle with my head, and soon I was standing on my head. After that, I stood on my head at every opportunity. I tried it one day when I was about forty – on the golf course – and I could still do it.

James wasn't very long with us before he emigrated to America, but he signed off with a flourish. One day I was helping him to bring in the hay from the meadows. We had just got a new hay float, which was a flat low wooden platform with shafts for the horse to pull it and a big cog wheel at the side with wire ropes to wind the cock of hay onto the float. This was a big advance, because previously we had to pitch the hay onto a cart which was very labour intensive. So James and I hopped on the float, James whistling as usual, and went to the Brilla to bring in the last load of the evening. We were just fitting the wire ropes around the bottom of the hay cock when we heard a shout from the river and James went down to investigate while I stayed to mind the horse.

People with meadows further along brought their load along the river bank because it was more level, except for one place where the only way through was very close to the river, with uneven ground sloping down towards the bank. It was a dangerous place and with the high load of hay it was very risky. That gap could have been made safe with a spade and an hour's work but nobody bothered. Paddy McCann, who didn't have a float, was coming with a top heavy load of hay and when he came through the gap, it keeled over into the river.

When James arrived at the spot, everything was on its side in the water with the horse being strangled in the harness. He and Paddy managed to cut the horse free but when it got free it struck out for the opposite bank, which was too high for it to climb on to.

So James took off his shoes and swam across, got the reins in his teeth and swam back again with the horse behind him. It was a very brave action, because those big hooves were pounding very close to him. The bank was much lower on our side of the river and when James got back with the horse, the two men were able to lead it out safely onto the bank.

When asked about it afterwards, James just said, "I used my side stroke," as if everybody should know that nothing would catch him with his side stroke. It was an act of great bravery. He and a few others used to swim in the canal at the high bridge and it was deep enough there for diving and James was indeed a very good swimmer. It was lucky that he was there.

He did come back from America about twenty years later on a holiday, but I didn't see him. He was a hero all right, when hero meant something. Not like today, when people are called heroes for doing their job.

A year or two after that, Charlie arrived – a middle aged man who was like a father to us, especially to Shamey. Shamey loved Charlie, and each Sunday, at King's Island chapel, the two of them would be seen standing together chatting, and that continued until Charlie retired many years later.

In the summer, when he arrived at eight o'clock in the morning, he would hang his jacket on a nail beside the stable door and when we got up to start getting ready for school we would run down to look in Charlie's coat pocket, where there would be a few lovely sweet apples from Charlie's garden.

He was our friend and mentor and he knew how to handle young lads. If we were gathering potatoes in the cold frosty mornings, no matter how many clothes we had on we would still be cold, especially our hands. Charlie was all right, because he was digging with the spade, but we stood there picking up the cold spuds and our little fingers were numb. But Charlie would start, "I remember one day me and Harry McCormack were on the three o'clock shift," and he would start to tell a long story of his life down the coal mines in Scotland, because that's where he had worked before. It was only in later years that I realised that he was just keeping our minds off the mind and body numbing job that we were doing.

In the early years when he finished work he came in and had his tea at six o'clock and then settled back to smoke his pipe. Shamey would climb on his knee and Charlie would stay with us, probably until about nine or ten o'clock, and then off he would go home and be back in the morning at eight. I never wondered then what his wife thought about that, but they seemed to get on all right.

Charlie was a steady, hard-working man, but he was a great talker. If he met someone on the road he would forget himself, especially if they were discussing the war. So, if he had a wheelbarrow, he wouldn't put it down on the ground, but would adopt a kangaroo squat with the handles of the wheelbarrow on each knee. In his mind he wasn't idling and he could stand like that for ages. I think he lost track of the time altogether.

He had a cure for everything. For a boil, of which there were a lot at that time, it was onions. To kill a tree it was bore a hole in the trunk and put a clove of garlic into it. I tried that recently and it didn't work. He would always say, "That's the foremost cure." He showed us how to set snares for rabbits and hares and even for rats, which was ingenious, because the rat would be left hanging in the air like on a gallows. I'm sure it would work, although I never tried it. I probably would have done so if I could have sold them for a shilling a piece.

When Charlie retired we all missed him, not only because he was a steady worker, but also because he had become part of the family.

CHAPTER THREE

L ife, when I think about it, was really quite primitive in my childhood: we had no electricity, no running water and outside toilets, the chemical type if you were so lucky. The roads were just rough cut stones and people in the bogs had ramparts made of soft moss where the turf was stacked to dry. These ramparts were lovely to walk on in the summertime but were mostly flooded during the winter months, hence it was a precarious existence in the bogs at that time.

Nearly everyone was honest and those that were not were well known. Everybody's door was open and people usually walked in and sat down.

We carried our drinking water from a communal pump at the corner. The handle had to be pumped up and down and was quite stiff. Frances would bring two buckets of water down in the morning and fill the crock in the scullery.

A family lived beside the pump and their mother was called Rosina. She wasn't very strong and I think she relied on Frances to pump the water. So as Frances walked past her window, sometimes very quietly if she was in a hurry, she'd hear the little ones shouting, "Fassy's at the pump, Fassy's at the pump, Mammy," and out they would come with pans and buckets to fill. When Frances was busy she was really annoyed.

Rosina was a great dressmaker and was very much used for altering hand-me-downs. My mother had one of her coats altered for me. It was brown and had a sprung waist. What I looked like I can't imagine, but in the country nobody cared.

Everyone seemed to know each other's business and nothing was private. I remember a young chap called John Joe got a new pair of dungarees. They were much too long, as all dungarees seemed to be at that time, and had to be altered by Rosina. Next thing I knew we were running behind him singing, "Big dungarees, Big dungarees. Go to Rosina's and get them sewn up, Big dungarees."

Frances lived with her uncle Jemmy Campbell and Aunt Kate on a small holding that was mostly moss and yielded good black turf, which Jemmy saved and sold in the towns and houses, where it was much appreciated.

Jemmy was a real character. He always wore a hard hat, both in winter and summer, and was known as 'The Hat' or, occasionally, 'Jemmy the Hat'. They lived on the main road to Coalisland and their hobby was noting every car or vehicle that passed by, and they wouldn't rest until they had identified any strange car that they saw.

"That's a traveller going to Magennis," Frances would say.

"The divil blow me, it didn't stop," Kate would say, scratching madly at a hole in her cap whenever she had a problem.

Jemmy had a habit of making a noise with his lips expelling air – "Buh, buh, buh," he would say. And sometimes he would say "bhuh" more quickly.

When he set off for Dungannon on a frosty still morning, we could hear the horse's shoes striking the road, the cartwheels rattling and Jemmy going, "Buh, buh, bhuh," until he went over the high bridge across the canal and the sound faded away.

"That car went down the other day," said Frances. "And Mrs. McCann's expecting."

"The divil blow me, you could be right," said Kate. "It would be that new Dr. O'Kane."

"Buh, bhuh," said Jemmy. "Wet that girl." That was his way of requesting his tea.

Kate also made a murmuring sound like she was humming a tune very low. Jemmy and Kate were quite a duet. We could walk in anytime and would always be welcome. They were very kind to us.

On Sunday morning, a card school took place in Jemmy's cart house. The cart was sitting with the shafts on the ground and the regulars were not all neighbours for some came from a mile or two away. Jemmy, wearing his hard hat, would sit on the middle of a shaft and the game, which was played with five cards, was called '15'. The ace of hearts was the best card in the pack, followed by the deuce. Three tricks won the game and each trick counted five.

About eight or nine players gathered around a piece of board between the shafts, and when they started playing the cards came flying around and around without a pause to take the tricks. It was a non-stop fast game, because whenever the trick was won the dealer immediately played the next card, without the tricks being lifted, and away they went again until the last card had been played.

Then Jemmy would say, "Buh, huh. Scowld the game," and everyone would call out his score.

"I'm a trick."

"I'm ten."

And so on, until a discrepancy would appear and the arguments would start. Once it was sorted out maybe a second argument would take place.

"Why did you hang my king? You shouldn't have hung my king." I never knew what that meant.

The scores were sorted out and if there was no winner, the cards were dealt again and started flying around with the same speed, until someone won and they all threw their hands in in disgust.

I never knew how games started at school or who started them. Suddenly every spring we were all playing marbles and for a hectic few weeks that was all that mattered. Then as suddenly as it had started, it stopped and we were then into hopscotch, which we called bedsies. When that was over the skipping ropes would appear.

We had a game called 'Draw a bucket of water'. I think four would hold hands and chant, "Draw a bucket of water, to drown a lady's daughter, one in a rush, two in a bush, please young lady step under," and we would lift our joined hands and bring someone from behind us. We would repeat the song until everyone was inside then we would jump up and down shouting, "A bag of rags, a bag of rags," and we would all fall down laughing. I don't know the meaning of that one.

Another game we had was called 'Cat and Bat'. This was played with a stick, like an officer's baton, cut out of the hedge, which we called the bat, and the cat was a stick of similar thickness about five inches long and sharpened at both ends like a pencil. All that was required now was a brick on which to lay the cat, with its end a couple of inches over the edge of the brick. The idea was to be 'in' and hit the cat with the bat. The cat would fly through the air and everyone waiting would jump to catch it. If it was cleanly caught then you were out and the catcher was in. Of course, you could hit it long or short, or you could place it on the brick to go high or low, and the catchers would place themselves wherever they fancied. It was a terrific game and cost nothing. I think the EU would probably ban it now on health and safety grounds. Politics!

My earliest childhood memories are vague, which is normal, as we tend not to remember very much from our youngest years. However, when I was still very young I do remember that Eileen Hughes started a camogie team.

Camogie is a game played in Ireland by ladies. Men also play a similar game, called Hurling; in Scotland it is called Shinty. Hurling is very popular in the South and draws capacity crowds to Croke Park in Dublin for the All Ireland semi finals and the finals. At the time, the GAA – Gaelic Athletic Association – was encouraging teams to form in the country districts so Eileen took up the task of introducing camogie to Derrytresk and surrounding areas.

First of all she organised collections in the district. I think everyone contributed and soon she had enough capital to purchase the equipment needed. Many people, especially men, treated it all as a joke, however, thanks to Eileen's efforts, the Derrytresk camogie team became a reality and the players were soon giving good account of themselves against other teams in the league.

I, being very young, just heard people talking about it and I heard that Tarry's Brita and Rose Fitzgerald on one particular Sunday had been the best players on the pitch.

Eileen didn't play – I don't think she had ever played the game – but she was captain and treasurer and walked round carrying a camogie stick. I can imagine she was an imposing figure on the sidelines. From nothing she had created a team and it was a success to the ladies of the district, but some men took a different view.

One Sunday, three men from Derrytresk football team called on Eileen and asked her could she loan them money, because Derrytresk was short of funds and couldn't fulfil their match commitments. She must have been very naïve, because she gave them the money and they, and I suppose the rest of the team, went straight to the pub and drank it all.

I heard people telling how the footballers were enjoying themselves in the pub by toasting the people whose money they were now spending.

"Here's to Ann Doyle's sixpence," they would say as they downed another whiskey.

The camogie team died. To the ladies of the district it was a sad loss; to the men, sadly, I think it was a bit of a giggle. Nowadays, women are more emancipated, we hope.

The fall of the camogie team didn't knock Eileen off her stride. She was nothing if not resilient. First she had been the nurse to Margaret and Eleanor Johnson of Lurgan, and when she called in to see my mother, Margaret and Eleanor would be the chief topic of conversation. Photos would be produced and their progress relayed to my mother and sometimes they would come down to visit her. She was very fond of those two girls. Then, when she moved to Captain Carson's house, the standards didn't drop, and I think Eileen absorbed a lot of the life that was led by those two families, adapting it to her own.

So it was no surprise to anyone when she announced that she was giving a party for the poor of the parish. When we found that we were being included in the poor we were very pleased, and when we saw that the teacher's two grandsons had been invited as well, we were surprised but happy.

What I recall about the party isn't very much. I know that we had lots of lemonade and cakes and chocolates. There was no ice cream because there was no electricity out in the country, Coalisland being the nearest place with electricity. Anyone who could sing or recite a poem was called upon to do so. I must have enjoyed it, as I remember coming home and telling everyone about it.

Probably, my earliest memory, apart from being lifted up to see the floods, was playing with Kathleen, which I think we did a lot. I remember playing on the loft steps which were typical of the time, just eight or nine steps and a landing, but without a hand rail, which was really quite dangerous. The reason I remember this evening is because we fought and I bit Kathleen on the wrist, and she still has the scars to this day.

She got her own back soon afterwards, though not intentionally, of course. We were getting ready to play Cat and Bat and Kathleen was sharpening the end of a piece of stick with the bread knife. I was standing in front of her and stuck out my finger to point to where to cut and she cut my knuckle, instead. It was a deep wound and I remember screaming. Of course, my mother would have had the iodine out and onto the cut in a flash, and that was worse. I still have the scar – one inch long – so we both bear the marks of battle. I think it was the four year difference in our ages that made us play together, as Elizabeth, who was just two years older than me, would not have been up to playing with a boy who was boisterous at an early age, I think.

Later on, though, it was with Elizabeth that I first tried to learn to ride a bicycle – a great challenge when we were young. I'm not aware that any bicycles were made for children then. If they were, it would have been for rich people who could afford them.

We were lucky in that everyone who came to the shop came on a bicycle and it was leaning against the wall while they were inside. So when we saw a lady's bike we tried to ride it down the road, one foot on the pedal and the other pushing along the road. Some people were not pleased, others were more tolerant.

Most of the ladies' bikes were the sit up and beg type, with very high handle bars, and it must have been laughable, if you were not the bike owner, to see us stretching up to the handle bars and beating the ground with our left foot.

There was one man, called Terence McCann, who didn't seem to mind at all and he used his wife's high handle bar bike. Up and down the road we went, my sisters and myself, and the joy we felt if we got the left foot up even for a few yards. However, we were continually ending up in the hedge, or worse, on the road. We realised we had to get up some speed in order to have enough time to get on and keep going, so we tried it very bravely on the hill past our house, with disastrous results.

Then we decided to go to Joe O'Neill's brae further along, which was a very gentle slope but was out of sight of the shop, and we would be in trouble if Daddy should find out. We took Terence's bike, and I held it for my sister Elizabeth, and then pushed her a bit as she wobbled but, sure enough, she moved down the little hill to shouts and screams from both of us. When it was my turn I, too, managed to ride for a bit. Terence was at the corner looking for us and didn't say a cross word. After that, no bike was safe – not even men's.

Elizabeth and I were a daft pair and we had a lot of fun in our teens. She taught me to dance, up in the loft with a hurricane lamp perched on a bag of cattle feed.

One, two, three; one, two, three, at first, round and round for the Waltz, and then, after that, the Foxtrot. We were both crazy about Bing Crosby, Ella Fitzgerald and Perry Como. When *Housewives' Choice* would be on the radio in the morning, I would be milking and Elizabeth would be in the kitchen and when a new tune came on she would shout down to me.

One morning, Ella Fitzgerald came on singing her latest hit, "My Happiness". She shouted, "Arthur, 'My Happiness'."

I left the cow and bucket and raced up to the kitchen. My father happened to be coming down from the shop as I went flying past him. He looked at the stool under the cow and the bucket, half full of milk, and he said to my mother, "Saviour God, did you ever see anything like that in your life?"

But, what could I do? "My Happiness" came first and in a few minutes I was back under the cow, probably singing it to her.

After all, we were a musical family. Kathleen and Mary went to Coalisland for piano lessons once a week. They got off school an hour early and went with the bread man, Mickey Madden, who called at the school for them. The music teacher was called Miss Waters. Kathleen and Mary walked home from Coalisland after their music lesson and they were very scared of a tall man called Pat English who stood outside his house every evening when they were passing. Of course, they thought he was waiting for them and crept or ran past him but, I suppose, he didn't even notice them. Each Monday evening we would hear about another narrow escape.

Kathleen showed great promise as a musician and Miss Waters sang her praises. "She has the touch," she would tell my mother. She did well in her exams, and Miss Waters entered her for a prestigious competition in Belfast. Incidentally, Miss Waters was a Protestant.

Kathleen was about twelve years old at the time and, when she finished her playing, there was a great burst of applause, and everybody went crowding around Miss Waters congratulating her. Of course, they took no notice of the child. Children were of no account then; it was all about the teacher.

Then a man came to Kathleen to take notes and asked her what she intended doing. She told him innocently enough that she was going to a boarding school in a convent. Soon after that, she discovered that the prize had been awarded to the second girl who was a Protestant.

At school we were taught that it was most important to be a Catholic, because otherwise one would go to Hell, which was a terrible fate. As I took it all very seriously, I was worried about Miss Waters, and I asked my mother one day, "Mammy, will Miss Waters go to Hell when she dies?"

"If she is good, she won't go to Hell," she replied.

I was relieved, but still puzzled.

Mary, also, won a prize when she was at the convent, but it was a gold medal for coming first in Northern Ireland in religious knowledge. That gold medal sat in a little box on the piano at home until I left. I suppose it's lost now.

Both Kathleen and Mary went to the convent boarding school and there was great excitement when they were coming home for the holidays in summer and for Christmas. My father harnessed the horse and trap, which had soft rubber hooped wheels and was as comfortable as a car with cushioned seats, and Jim, our horse, was dressed in his best gleaming harness.

We would wait to collect them off the bus at Tamnamore corner and the fun would begin. When we got home, Kathleen would make straight for the piano and that's where she practically lived for the next two months. The music she played was swing and jazz. She could make that piano bounce.

She could also play the cello and was in the orchestra at the convent, where they performed musicals – she taught me Gilbert and Sullivan operas that they had done that term.

I remember one holiday she had the music with her for "Lullaby of Broadway", which was a hit at the time, and how she could play it! We could hear her out on the road when we were going past. I can still hear her now, and when I think of it, it's not long before my foot starts tapping.

CHAPTER FOUR

After school one day I went with Frances to milk the black cow which was left alone in the fenced meadow in the Brilla and had to be milked every afternoon. We were walking along the main thoroughfare called the Brilla rampart – Frances carried her pail in one hand and held my hand with her other. We had just turned a bend in the rampart and were walking through a damp patch where the rushes were taller than I was because I could see the little clusters of seeds at eye level. Frances started to sing "The old pals are always the best you see", which was a popular Jimmy Rogers song at the time.

"That's wrong," I said to Frances, then sang the same line again going a tone higher on the final note.

"Do you think so?" said Frances, then she said, "What day is this, Arthur?"

"It's Wednesday," I replied.

"No, but what date is it?"

"It's the fourteenth of June," I said, then screamed, "It's my birthday!" and I let her hand go and took off through the rushes. In my bare feet and along the soft moss road I ate up the distance and burst into the shop to tell my father, the custom being that I was given a bottle of lemonade and a lot of creamy biscuits to celebrate with. That was 1933 and I was seven years old.

The Magennis Family around 1933
(The baby, Peggy, isn't on the picture.) Left to Right:
Back Row: Mary, 13, Kathleen, 11, Elizabeth, 9.
Front Row: James (father), Shamey, 3,
Arthur, 7, Teresa (mother).

Birthdays were celebrated like that, with lemonade, biscuits and cakes, and we had little parties. But apart from Father Christmas, who never forgot us, there wasn't any custom of buying or giving presents.

Christmas, like everywhere, was exciting for a child. We wrote our note and left it on a ledge up the chimney – in the soot – as it was an open hearth. I particularly remember checking when I came home from school and finding that he hadn't called. This worried me a lot and my mother assured me that he would call that night, and sure enough he did.

On Christmas morning my stocking would contain, in the toe, a penny and an orange, other little things like sweets and, glory be, a horse, which couldn't get into my stocking but was attached. One year I got a wind-up creamery cart in which the horse would run forward, buck in the air and then run backward. That was the greatest present I ever got from Santa. God bless him.

At Christmas we also got presents from the reps who called on us throughout the year. The best presents, as far as us children were concerned, were those from the sweet and chocolate reps. Miss McCauley, who I think was a director of the company, came from Portadown and would arrive down at our house with big boxes of chocolate tied with beautiful ribbons. When she left, the table in the parlour where my mother put them looked like Aladdin's cave. Then there was the tea rep and the cigarette rep and others who would bring individual presents for us. Someone once brought me a cricket bat and ball. I had no idea what cricket was, as we only played Gaelic football, so the bat and ball just lay there untouched for a long time. Another present was a tennis racquet but that wasn't any use either, as the nearest tennis courts would probably be in Dungannon, seven miles away.

On Christmas Eve it was the custom for shops to give presents to their customers. My father gave each customer a quarter of tea and a pound of sugar. These weren't packed as they are today, but had to be weighed out separately from the tea chest and the sack. This was a lot of extra work and my father had to have extra help. My mother said that people came whom she hadn't seen from the year before, and some would go to another grocer and maybe two if they were hard-faced enough. But it was only once a year and it wouldn't do to refuse them in front of a shop full of customers.

One year a young man called Dermot O'Neill came from Belfast to stay at Hughes'. He was probably in his teens and when he saw the cricket bat and ball, he decided to instruct me in the rules of the game. We went into the garden and he bowled and I batted, then I bowled and he batted but when he left a short time later, the bat and ball just lay around and were forgotten.

While he was staying at Hughes', Dermot came with me in the cart one day when I was delivering a small sack of flour to a customer. I think he knew as little about a horse as I knew about cricket. I took the flour into the customer's house and I left Dermot in the cart minding the horse. I heard the horse and the cart take off and on running out I discovered that the horse, which was skittish, had run away. I yelled at him to grab the reins but he grabbed the horse's tail instead and leaned back pulling with all his might. I think that the horse was so shocked that he stopped about fifty yards along and all was well.

The house where I delivered the flour belonged to Mrs. Ann Doyle. James Pat was her son and he was a cobbler. We took our boots to him to be mended and when we called back for them he was invariably behind time but he would say, "They're nearly ready, just sit down for a minute." He was usually laughing and he would start on the shoes while we watched. He was surrounded by lots of shoes, either repaired or waiting to be repaired, and sparbles, which are little nails that are hammered into the sole so that we were walking on sparble heads instead of leather. Sparbles littered the floor and on top of all a great piece of leather which must have been one side of a cow.

Sitting up on his stool in the middle of this, he would grab the leather, which was very stiff and difficult to control, and manhandle it onto his knee, where he would cut a piece from it with his very sharp cobbler's knife. He would shove the large piece of leather away from him and it would spring away onto the top of the pile like a live thing. Then at last we saw our boots when he reached into the pile and found them first time.

He placed the leather on the boot sole and, tacking it to the sole of the shoe, he cut around it and the outside piece fell onto the floor on top of a little mound of pieces. All the time he was laughing and joking and singing this song:

When my wife dies I'll get another one
A big tall yellow one just like the other one.

When the piece of leather was fitted to his satisfaction he would put it on the last and hammer in a row of rivets around the edge, which he took out of his mouth,. Then he took the sparbles and hammered them into the sole in a pattern. Next he went around the edges with black wax and our boots looked like new. It was fascinating to watch and I asked him for a piece of the off-cut leather, which was about two or three inches long and he gave it to me and said, "What do you want that for?"

I didn't know myself. I think it was the smell of it and I kept it in my pocket for ages.

After that, I decided I was going to be a cobbler. I told my mother and father but they took no notice, however, Charlie, as usual, was much more understanding and would say, "Aye, aye, aye," as if he understood perfectly.

I told Charlie that I was not going back to school and we discussed where I would have my cobbler's shop and Charlie said, "Aye, aye," and I knew he was in full agreement.

I thought about nothing else for a while. Nothing seemed to matter except this one ambition and yet it passed and the next thing was that I wanted to be a carpenter, after having woodwork lessons at school, so Charlie had to go through it all again. I told him I was going to get a chisel and Charlie said, "Get a Mathieson chisel because it's the best chisel," and I persuaded my mother to buy me one.

I still have an urge to make things, to cut and fit things together, and writing this gives me the same satisfaction; fitting sentences together is perhaps similar.

When I was about ten or eleven, a gang of lads would appear each Sunday morning going past our house with their dogs on their way to the canal to hunt water hens. My mother was over careful with me, I thought, and she didn't like me going to the river or the canal, but when the gang of hunters, all about my age, arrived I had to join them, no matter what.

54

I had a little white prayer book and I used it to coax Paddy the Guy's big brown dog, Tray, away with us, as he had a powerful nose and was a great hunter. I don't think it would have been any good without him. When we reached the canal we went along the meadow side, the opposite side to the towpath, as it was thick with reeds and great cover for water hens.

Tray and the other dogs would run along the edge until they saw or scented a water hen and they would go splashing in after it. It would either dive, in which case they would go paddling around looking for it, or it would fly away into the trees on the other side and we'd chase it for a bit, screaming and shouting and, if someone had a catapult, they would lose a fusillade of pebbles at it, which didn't reach halfway.

All together that's what we did, mostly a lot of shouting and screaming and running. We all followed behind Tray, because his keen nose would pick up a scent, and then he would stand still like a pointer and, suddenly, he would plunge and the water hen would either dive or take off followed by a crowd of us shouting and screaming again.

On considering it now, why should we hunt these birds which are inedible and uncatchable? I think it was just children playing. We certainly enjoyed it and came home on Sunday afternoon worn out but happy. I've never heard of hunting water hens before or since then. I think some bright spark must have done it by chance and enjoyed it so much he told all the others and a new sport was born.

Afterwards, I returned Tray to Paddy the Guy, a character who was a permanent fixture at Hughes'. He didn't live there but in what was left of a house belonging to Mrs. Hughes. It was just one bay that was still standing, well thatched and comfortable enough. It was about half a mile from Hughes' and he had to go past our house, morning and night, on his journey every day. The problem was that he could barely walk. Arthritis had him crippled. He was bent over and he used a very short stick to walk. His stride was about one foot long and he took about one hour to walk that half mile night and morning. He always had his dog with him and it would toddle along beside him, taking one or two steps and waiting. They were both an example of extreme patience.

When his dog was young he would go running after his tail, as dogs do. He'd go round and round so fast that he would fall in a pile on the road and Paddy informed us that he thought he had a worm in his tail. So, his first remedy was to shave the dog's tail and for weeks the dog went around shaved down to the skin. He must have shaved it every day but the dog still chased his tail.

Paddy decided that he would sting the dog's tail with nettles and the nettle acid would kill the worm. After that, the dog's tail was red, as Paddy probably stung it every morning, but he stopped chasing it. I think he broke the habit and the Guy thought he had killed the worm.

Why did Paddy the Guy live where he did when Peter would have kept him at home, I'm sure? I think he liked his privacy. In his house he had a bucket of clean water from the nearby well, a piece of sacking hanging on a nail in the fireplace where he kept his loaf, a mug and a knife and a little table beside him, and he could make tea and eat his bread without having to get up. His bed was on the other side of the room and the dog slept beside the bed.

I think he also had his pride. After he arrived at Hughes' in the morning and had his breakfast, he would go out with his dog to the back garden and work all day. The back garden was a small orchard and between the rows of apple trees, Paddy planted rigs of early potatoes. He had a very short, sharp spade and would dig that garden, manure it, plant the potatoes and eventually harvest them. All this at a snail's pace.

Paddy loved to sing. He had a powerful voice and on a frosty still morning we could hear him almost as soon as he left the house, which was at eight o'clock.

When my sister Mary was ill, Paddy would stand outside our front gate or, rather he had a way of sitting on his stick, and sing a song for her. Sometimes he would call in and say, "I sang one for you this morning, Minnie," and she would say, "Oh, it was lovely, Paddy, thank you."

It seems that he had been a heavy drinker at one time, and would have been found lying in the ditch frozen in the wintertime, and that is how he became arthritic. My sister Elizabeth said he had eyes like John Wayne and was quite handsome, but then she is a romantic soul.

Paddy paid his way no matter what cost to himself – he never complained and laughed and sang and told jokes, and who knows what he suffered; an example of patience and fortitude to us all.

Upstairs in Hughes' outside barn lived Tom McAtarseny, an old man who climbed up a wooden ladder to the barn every night, and somehow got down again in the morning. He would help out around the place but I never knew the explanation for his presence. He probably just came along one day and stayed. He was simply a quiet old man with whom we chatted occasionally. He had a great love for cats and if he was in the kitchen having his porridge, he would be surrounded by kittens, which he would feed by putting down his milky porridge on the sandstone tiles that had worn away in places to form saucers. When he went out the cats followed and I wouldn't be surprised if they slept with him.

Growing up on a farm, children always want to do things that grown-ups do. Milking a cow was one of those things and when the eldest was able to milk, we all wanted to milk but the forearm muscles were not developed enough and we were glad to stop trying very quickly.

Kathleen was the first to master the art and then she was allocated an easy cow to milk each night. At first, she was pleased and felt very grown up but, alas, the novelty soon wore off and it became a chore.

There were cows which were easier to milk and we always learned on those. There were also dangerous cows that would kick so we had to be taught how to cope with them. Don't walk too closely behind the cow, or horse, as it could break your leg or worse with a kick. Also, beware of a side swipe when milking. The best way to do it with a young cow, or a cow you can't trust, was to put your head against its flank, as this hampers a side swipe.

But cows usually settle down to a new milker and will get attached to them.

In the summer we milked the cows outside, thus saving a lot of work driving them in, cleaning them, putting them out to the field and cleaning the byre. I remember I used to milk a newly calved heifer that was very placid and became a pet. It got so attached to me that when the cows were in the field along the road, it would walk along the hedge when I was going to the shop, mooing at me through the holes in the hedge and, sometimes, waiting to walk back again. I think as its calf was taken away and I took its place, I became a substitute calf.

CHAPTER FIVE

L adies delight – first in the morning and last at night."

That was the greeting that came from Jack Smith, a travelling salesman who burst into our kitchen while we were having breakfast one morning. He was brandishing a large pink and white chamber pot and there was no doubt that we were gobsmacked for about ten seconds before we saw the humorous side.

Jack was indeed a character who looked like James Cagney, the film star. He was funny and got on well with everyone. On another morning he came in about the same time and one of us was crying, perhaps Peggy, who was the baby of the family.

He stood looking at her and said, "Why are you crying? I'm Jack Smith, all the way from Portadown and I haven't cried yet."

We had many travelling salesmen who came our way, especially in the summertime. Some had transport but most of them got off the bus at Tamnamore and walked carrying big suitcases loaded with their wares.

Each summer there would be Indians, whom we called Darkies, who always had huge cases and would toil up our hill in the hot sunshine carrying their heavy loads. I always felt sorry for them but, I suppose, they were more used to the heat than we.

They would call in our house and proceed to cover our kitchen with beautiful coloured silks of all hues and sizes.

"No buy, missus," they would say.

My mother would make them a cup of tea and I can't remember whether she bought anything or not. I suppose she bought something – a silk headscarf, perhaps, as they were quite popular then.

Then the Darkie would patiently pack everything back again. We called them Darkies as the most convenient term to describe them as they were darker than us. There was no colour bar in Derryvarn and we didn't think of ourselves as any better or any worse than the Darkies.

Years later in the 1950s, when I was working in a chemist's shop in Birmingham, an Indian packman came in and I invited him into the dispensary where he displayed his wares. I had no interest in his silks but I bought an eternity ring from him, as I was recently married and I thought my wife would like it. However, she wasn't very taken with it so I put it in the shop window and sold it. The Indian had a cup of tea and off he went. I suppose he was quite pleased with his sale and probably with his reception.

When I was very young, an old man lived across the road from our shop called Peter Gartland. He had a nice little farm which he and his brother, Larry, worked. He was a bit of a character and was forever giving my father the benefit of his theories on economics.

"What, what, what?" he would say. "You feed a hen for a penny a day and she will lay an egg for a penny a day. Where is the profit? Where is the profit? What, what, what?"

A small farmer's life in the 1930s was not easy. Hay sheds, those large structures with rounded roofs, built from corrugated zinc which are a common site at every farm today, would not been seen in the late 1920s and early 1930s, except in large farms.

Farms in Ireland were owned by the farmers, not like in England where they were leased from huge estates. The hay, when it was drawn home in the autumn would be built in hay stacks called packs in the haggard, or hay yard. These packs were shaped like the cocks of hay in the meadow and it took about ten cocks of hay, I think, to make one pack.

Peter Hughes was a remarkable cock and pack builder for his age. He could stand at the top putting little bits of hay under his feet with the end of a rake which he held in one hand and would tramp, tramp, tramp with his feet and pat, pat, pat with the butt end of his rake until there was only room at the top for his two feet. Then, rake in hand, he would slide to the ground like a young man but probably more gracefully.

At harvest time Peter, of course, built the packs and to see that old man up there with two men pitching the hay to him with long forks, was worth watching. As the packs got higher, the pitchers would have to climb ladders to reach up to the builder. That wasn't easy and after a first day of pitching hay the muscles would be groaning next morning.

The pack of hay would be as tall as some of the trees around it. The trees were planted there to provide shelter when the gales would blow in the winter, and the packs would be roped with grass rope, which we sold in the shop. The grass rope would be put over the top and a brick tied to the bottom on each side. Then another grass rope would be put about three feet from the first and so on around the pack.

The reason the grass ropes were not tied to the pack was because as the hay was pulled from the pack every morning and evening to feed the cattle and horses, the pack shrunk and during the winter months the grass rope would have become loose and the first gale would have lifted the hay and blown it away. But the bricks kept the ropes taut.

When a farmer got up in the morning, his first job was to feed the stock. He would boil a kettle for his tea and in the press he would find a large griddle-sized soda bread. He would tear off a piece and sit down with his tea and that would keep him going until breakfast. Soda bread would fill him and he wouldn't be hungry, whereas, if he had a slice of white bread from a loaf, he would be starving in a short time.

As soon as the livestock heard his feet they set up a chorus – cows, young calves and horses all at the same time. He would start pulling hay from the pack and carrying it into the byre, as large an armful as he could carry between each pair of cows in the byre, because each stall held two animals. Then he would fill the horses' manger. Next he would start the milking because the creamery man would come later with his horse and cart to pick up his milk churns, and then he would have his breakfast.

The packs of hay were measured by leaning against the pack while facing it with outstretched arms and going around the pack and counting how many stretches were needed to circumnavigate the pack. A pitchfork was first placed at the spot you started so you counted until you reached the pitchfork when you came round again. This was called a faddam, which I suppose meant a fathom.

Jemmy Hat used to buy hay and one day when he came to measure the pack, or faddam, as he would say, he placed his fork against the pack and started to faddam. When he came round again to where he had started he stood looking for a while at the man who was selling the hay. The man had been standing where Jemmy had placed the pitchfork, and the Hat had a turn in his eye so it was difficult to tell if he was looking at the man or over his shoulder.

Eventually, he said, "Buh, buh. I'll faddam it again and this time you come with me to make sure I'm not cheating." A very subtle way of informing the man that he didn't trust him and thought that the pitch fork may have been moved. The Hat was an old hand and he could estimate roughly how much hay was in the pack just by observation.

One hot summer day, Peter Gartland, our neighbour across the road, was drawing home the hay and building it in packs in the yard for the winter feed. When the job was finished, as was the custom, he sent down to the pub for whiskey to treat the men. Whiskey was quite a luxury then as not many people could afford the price. In a short time the men were all more or less drunk and they just stretched out on the grass along the roadside, and most of them fell asleep in the sun.

A travelling salesman who was coming to our shop and who was new to the district saw one of them lying in the grass and he asked him where Magennis's shop was. As he related to my father later, the man muttered, "Hup, hup," still talking to his horse, so the rep continued on his way until he came to another man lying in the grass and he asked him the same question. This man was lying on his side with one hand tucked into his trouser pocket and, without opening his eyes he pointed with his leg in the right direction and snored away. The traveller was disgusted.

"That is the laziest act I have ever seen. If you can show me a lazier act than that I'll give you a shilling," he said.

The man rolled a bit further over and raised his hand slightly to leave a space in his pocket and said, "Just drop it in there." I think the traveller paid up.

Peter Gartland had a black collie dog called Kruger after the South African general in the Boer war. This would be in the early thirties, so the Boer war would still be remembered. Peter died while I was very young. When somebody dies, the corpse is usually laid out on the bed in the room for two days and people call in to pay their respects. Peter was the first dead person I had seen and I remember it as quite a shock.

When we came home from school, myself and my sisters were sent to the burial house, as it was called, and we were told to go to the bedside, kneel down and pray for the repose of his soul, which we dutifully did, but I think I just stared at the yellowish sallow face and bony hands with the rosary beads entwined round the fingers.

All day long people came and went and then in the evening mostly men would come to the wake. Everyone would be offered refreshments: tea, whiskey, cigarettes. The corpse was not hidden away in a funeral parlour like it is now.

Another death I remember was Felix, the Alsatian, which belonged to Captain and Mrs. Carson, for whom Eileen Hughes worked. He was very old and very much valued by them, as he had apparently saved the Captain's life in China.

One night when I went into Hughes' there was a huge dog lying on his side on blankets in front of the fire. He was just skin and bones and Eileen was wiping away the phlegm from his mouth. The Carsons were on their summer vacation and Eileen was nursing the dog.

This dog got everything, including spoonfuls of brandy, and all sorts of medicines were provided, but he didn't last very long. Eileen looked after him like a child while regaling the ceilidhers with tales of his bravery.

The following spring a large mobile kennel arrived in Hughes' garden. It was placed facing the road with iron bars in the front and in it were four Alsatian pups. Eileen was now equipped with a new bicycle and a leather coat and all the accessories required by a dog handler. As the pups grew up they could see the road, and the noise they set up every time anyone went past was very bad. We used to bend down and tiptoe past, but it never worked.

They were thoroughbreds for showing and had names like Ajax of Brushwood, which amazed me as I had never heard names like that for a dog.

One wet afternoon, Eileen went past our house in her leather coat and on her new shiny bicycle with four pups on leads. How she ever got on the bike, I don't know, but she came off into the hedge at our house. Nothing serious, but that was the last we saw of the bike.

The dogs remained until the Carsons returned in the autumn and Eileen was given the largest of the litter, called Derry – a beautiful dog with a beautiful nature, but huge. She was also given a mini white smooth fox terrier bitch called Judy, who was about nine inches tall. The two pups were inseparable and looked so very funny running together, but the road became quiet and peaceful once more.

Derry, as in the name Derrytresk, comes from the Irish word for oak, because that part of Ireland was once covered by forests of mostly oak and fir. This accounts for the number of fir tree and black oak roots found in the moss. Now that the land is drained this causes some inconvenience to the farmers who, if they wish to cultivate the land, must run the gauntlet of having a plough get stuck into a great root, damaging the agricultural implement and, maybe, the horse or, later on, the tractors.

Some farmers got over this obstacle by using a piece of stick cut from the hedge to connect the plough to the horse or tractor, instead of the usual iron pin. When the sock of the plough struck a stump of the root, the wooden pin would break but the sock would get no harm.

This procedure was all explained to my sister, Elizabeth, who was in charge of the shop one rainy night about eleven o'clock, when a woman called Susan McCann arrived with her little girl on a donkey and cart for supplies. She had come a long way from the lough shore and was very wet when Elizabeth opened the shop for her. She told her that she was so late because they had been finishing the ploughing and had been held up by the oak stumps.

When she had her supplies in the cart she bought a bap and gave it to the little girl, saying, "Give that to him."

Elizabeth went to the window to look at who was outside as she hadn't seen anybody else before. The little girl went out with the bap and gave it to the donkey, which appeared very pleased and ate it all happily. The donkey was part of the family, it seemed.

Farmers were always trying to reclaim the land by removing the stumps altogether. This was very hard work but was made even more worthwhile by the value of the fir, which was much sought after as firelighters, as it contained a flammable resin. There were special fir axes made for splitting these roots into small pieces, which was also back-breaking work. On Saturday mornings, donkey and horse carts could be seen on the way to Coalisland to sell little bundles of fir firelighters around the houses in the towns.

It was quite easy to expose the fir and oak stumps, as the moss was soft and easily dug back to strip the roots of the stumps, which were several yards long and, maybe, running in different directions. They probably weighed about a ton but, as they were in the soft moss, a horse or tractor could not be used to haul the stumps out of the way.

On a number of occasions on the land adjacent to the school, the owner would borrow the children at lunchtime or just after school, to come down and pull on a long tether attached to the stumps. About twenty or thirty big lads and lasses would remove the log easily and pull it to a prepared spot. Anything that broke the monotony of school was enjoyable, especially if the tether slipped or broke and we'd all collapse laughing on top of each other.

CHAPTER SIX

My mother's hen turkey, which provided her with the eggs for hatching and rearing for Christmas, was the most cunning of birds. Like most hens, it wanted to lay its eggs somewhere very secluded. It would start disappearing in the spring and my mother would set me the task of following the turkey. At first I was baffled because the turkey would head east across a field followed by me at a discreet distance. It was in no hurry and would stop and peck and eat and then it would pass through a hedge into the next field and, if I couldn't get through quickly, it would disappear on the other side. Gradually, I discovered if the turkey headed east, then the nest was probably due west and it would walk half a mile in the wrong direction before doing a quick turn when it got into the next field. A smart walk along the hedge and another turn would find it on its way back to its nest.

Once I found its nest, if it was in a safe place, I would leave it alone until it brought its flock of day old turkeys back to mix with the other fowl.

When I was about ten years old, my mother hurt her leg badly on a zinc bucket. It left a huge gash and the doctor advised her that she must not stand on her leg for weeks, otherwise it would never heal. She devised a means of getting around the kitchen and

71

up and down to the bedroom by kneeling on a cushion on a chair with her bad leg and shuffling around. This seemed to work all right and I was kept at home from school, wonder of wonders, to do her running for her. Frances was there to do the heavier work and milk the cows, while I looked after the hens, gathered the eggs and fed the turkeys. I recall they were nearly fully grown, so it must have been about September.

There were tea chests turned upside down in the garden and the tall turkeys could reach up to eat the food that I would prepare for them and place on the top of each one. It was always made of 'Feed All', which was really turkey cornflakes, on which I poured boiling water and mixed up in a bucket into a turkey mash.

The turkeys loved it but, then, so did the hens. When I placed it on the top of the tea chest, the turkeys gathered around it and it was just the right height for them. But I had a few tea chests to attend to and those cheeky hens would fly up onto one of the tea chests when my back was turned and gobble up the turkeys' cornflakes. I would rush at one and dive at another but I was outnumbered. Then I decided I would punish each hen I caught by making an example of it in front of its friends.

There was a huge pot of rainwater about two feet in diameter with a lid. I would grab the offending hen, push her into the pot and put the lid on it. Then I would count slowly to impress the audience – I don't remember how long – then take off the lid and extract the bedraggled hen and put her down amongst the others. The poor thing must have been very nearly choked. I don't know how long I had been punishing the hens – perhaps, I had just started – but on the morning in question I looked up and there stood Frances on the road beside me, looking over the hedge, and quickly observing the whole drama.

Well, I was called many things that morning by my mother and Frances, asking, "How could I be so stupid?" which hurt as I thought I was truly inspired. Worse still, I was threatened with being sent back to school the next day. But this sentence was commuted to staying at home and being closely watched. I really enjoyed that time at home. I think it was because I was fully occupied all day – hens, eggs, turkeys, running up to the shop, bringing in a turnip or a cabbage from the field – and everything was done at the speed of light. It was great to be young.

While I'm on the subject of turkeys, there was a gentleman draper from Coalisland who would ride out on his bicycle in the spring and summer evenings and call on likely houses to see if he could measure a client for a new suit.

My father, who was always busy, didn't like him coming as he would stay for tea and my father would feel obliged to sit and talk with him when he would rather be getting on with one of his jobs.

One evening he called on my mother's sister, Aunt Maggie, also a farmer's wife, who looked out of the window and exclaimed to her daughter Mary, "Here comes the tailor. I don't want anything from him so I'll hide down the room. Tell him I'm out and get rid of him."

So Mary received him but it wasn't so easy getting rid of him and he lingered and talked in his slow way and asked, "How is Daddy and how is Mammy?"

Maggie, in the meantime, was in the bedroom, looking out of the window at her young turkeys, thinking how well they were doing when, suddenly, a cat appeared and grabbed one of them. Maggie pushed up the window and put her head out waving her arms and shouting, "Scat," and "Be off," and anything that came to mind. Then the window dropped onto her neck pinning her down so she couldn't move. All she could do was shout for help. She was overheard by Mary and released by none other than the suit man.

"Ah, how on earth have you got yourself in this predicament?"

Maggie was embarrassed, of course, but later she thought there might be a silver lining and maybe he wouldn't be in a hurry to come back again.

There was a lot of work to do around the farm and plenty to keep my mother and Frances occupied in the house. The milk churning, for example, took place every fortnight, I think. Two big crocks of milk would be left in the scullery to go sour. They were fitted with big wooden lids with handles. In the wintertime they would be brought into the kitchen and placed at the side of the fire, especially if the weather was frosty.

Churning day was a bit like washday because my mother and Frances would be busy and we didn't get our usual attention. The churn would be placed in the middle of the floor in the scullery, or in the kitchen in the wintertime, and the two crocks of thick sour milk emptied into it. Then the churn staff was put in and the lid put on the churn. The lid had a hole in the centre, through which the churn staff was pushed. At the bottom the churn staff had a round wooden platform about a foot wide which was full of round holes. The churner stood and lifted it up and down in a steady rhythm. It was hard work, but if it was lifted up and down from the waist, not just with shoulders, it was a lot easier. Of course, children couldn't do it and Frances and my mother took turns.

If a neighbour came in it was the custom to give you a "brash", that is about five minutes on the churn staff. When the milk broke, as it was called, we could tell by the sound, which became softer, then we might get a turn at gathering the butter. This was achieved by putting a turf under one side of the churn and gently rocking it from side to side. When the lid was taken off, the butter would be floating in one solid piece in the middle of the buttermilk. My mother would take it out with two wooden butter bats and finally it would be finished with a fancy design on it and it was delicious. As well as that, the fresh buttermilk was beautiful and we all loved to drink it if we were thirsty.

It was the routine of farm life that kept it running smoothly. The cows were taken down to the bog every day to graze. Of course, it was no longer a bog but once a name is given it sticks. In the summer holidays I loved taking them, especially on those hot sunny mornings. There was still a low lying piece of moss with many ponds and waterways in it and here we met the dragon flies, or devil's needles as we called them; hundreds of them darting here and there and everywhere. Some were a beautiful dark shiny blue, others red or green. Their colours were magnificent but when I was small I was scared of them as they would fly up in front of my face and then stop dead as if they were daring me to move.

When the cows entered the bog and I had closed the gate again, I was then free to go to the blayberry patch just along the top of our bog. It was a dry bank and it was covered with blayberries. I sat in there and ate all I could hold, and they were beautiful. Then maybe I would lie on my back and look at the sun for a long time until it would turn into a black ball. I think that's maybe why I finished up with glaucoma, as one should never look directly at the sun – but I did.

We had lots of larks nesting in the heathery moss banks and they would take off with a burst of song and rise straight up until one lost sight of them. I would lie on my back in order to follow them, but eventually they would become a dot in the blue.

If they were disturbed on the nest they would run off at a tangent, trailing what I thought, at first, was a broken wing, but later discovered that this was a trick to lure me away from the nest. They were beautiful singing birds and we had lots of them. I had a bird cage and tried to cage them but, of course, they died.

In the summer months, Peter Hughes and I would go fishing on a Sunday morning. Straight across the meadows there was the style meadow along the river and this was supposed to be the best spot for catching fish. We occasionally caught a fish or two but we were not very successful. Peter would tell me that the weather was not favourable or something similar.

Then one morning we set off and Peter remarked that the wind was in the south and fish might bite. And, sure enough, they did. The river was full of bream, a big fish shaped like a saucer. Before this we had only been catching tench. We couldn't bait our hooks fast enough, and after about half an hour the biting stopped as suddenly as it had started. Peter caught twelve lovely bream and I caught eight. What a morning – and they tasted like fish should taste.

Another fishing morning I remember was once when there was no biting and a young lad can get very bored just sitting. We were fishing with our worm about twelve inches below the surface but nothing was happening. So I pulled mine out and put it about two feet deep. Then I had to do something different again, so I put my bait as deep as it would go, until it was probably lying on the bottom. Suddenly my cork bobbed up and down then disappeared under the water and I snatched my rod up and flicked it back onto the bank and there was a black snake, as I thought, wriggling through the grass.

I jumped up and ran but Peter shouted, "Holy boots, you've caught an eel."

It was about two feet long. It was my first taste of eel and was certainly worth waiting for. We skinned it and then hung the skin in the crook of the fire because when it was dry it could be used as a strap around the wrist or leg if anyone had a sprain. However, if this didn't make it better, you could always go to someone for 'the charm'.

In Ireland there are people who have a charm for a certain disease. This charm has been handed down through the generations. It is frowned upon by the Catholic Church but it goes back a long long way and people with a charm are very sincere about it. They do not accept any reward and if you gave them a reward then the charm would not work.

The first charm we came in contact with was when we were very young and got a stye, which we used to do quite often. My mother would send us down to Mrs. Hughes who had the charm for a stye. When we got there Mrs. Hughes would send us out to the gooseberry bushes to break off nine prickles and bring them to her. Then she would take the prickles and point each one in turn at the stye then throw each one over her shoulder and the job was done. I suppose the stye would have got better anyhow.

Once when I was playing football I went over on my ankle and it came up like a small loaf. I couldn't put my foot to the ground and my mother said to go down to Jane Donaghy who had the charm for a sprain. Having nothing else to do except sit in the house with my foot up, I was glad of the break. I must admit that I was an unbeliever but down I went to Jane, walking on a stick which took all the weight on that side. Jane got a potato, which she cut into a number of pieces, and then she rubbed each piece gently on my foot and put them back again on the table. She then gently caressed my ankle with her cool hands and, I must say, it was soothing.

"There," she said, "It will be better soon," so off I hobbled again. I had to pass Hughes' about fifty yards up the road and when I reached it I stopped to look up their street at I don't remember what, but it must have been interesting because I forgot about my foot and when I looked down I had my toes on the ground. As I walked home I was able to put a little weight on my toes. When I told my mother about it she just said, "I told you Jane would fix it for you."

"There are more things in heaven and earth, Horatio." Shakespeare said that, I think, meaning we don't know it all.

CHAPTER SEVEN

R eligion played a big part in our lives when we were young. When I sat on my mother's knee being dressed every morning I had my face washed and my hair combed. Then I had to say my prayers which were, "Mother Mary, Queen most sweet, Lead us safe to Jesus feet."

Then one morning I said, "I can say it, Mammy."

"All right, you say it," she said.

And I said, "Mother Mary, Queen most sweet, Lay an egg at Jesus feet," which shows the influence that hens already had on my life.

Hens wandered all over the farm until we eventually erected a pen. They would even sneak into the bedroom and lay an egg on the bed. Often we got a shock in the bedroom when suddenly we became aware of a beady eye watching us from the bed.

At school, when we were about seven years old, we prepared to make our First Communion. We rehearsed everything but first we had to go to confession and confess our sins to the priest. But we had to think of our sins ourselves.

So Saturday morning we all arrived at the church to go to confession. I don't remember anything about mine, but after we had all finished and were waiting to go home, one girl called Mary Ellen suddenly got up and marched back in again. She had forgotten a sin. Shock waves passed through us. Afterwards, although we had been told not to tell each other what we had confessed, some just couldn't keep it a secret. So the teacher's son Patsy told us that his sins were, "I fought with Tilly, I fought with Sean and I broke the leg of Biddy's duck." I don't think the Lord will ever forgive him for that.

Missionary preachers came about every two years to give us a couple of weeks hard praying and hard preaching. It seems we needed to have our fervour recharged. They had a good cop – bad cop routine. One would preach gently and softly and tell us God loved us all and we just must do our best to please Him. And the following evening his colleague would come thundering hell fire and damnation. He had a huge voice and he scared the living daylights out of me, as I took religion seriously at that time.

When we came out of the church the men usually stood around the entrance smoking. I used to be amazed that some people were not the slightest bit scared by it all. But I was.

One night the 'bad cop' had been preaching about impure thoughts. He meant those of a sexual nature, of course. He said the thought occurred in three stages and you were to get rid of it at the first stage, but certainly no further than the second. Afterwards, I was standing next to a man called Alec, just lighting up a cigarette, who was very witty. A pretty girl walked past him.

He turned to me and said, "That was close, Arthur. I was just in the second stage of a bad thought." I laughed and suddenly it wasn't so much doom and gloom as before.

Before the missions started one of the priests told us that they would endeavour to visit each house, and to facilitate this he asked people not to offer them tea or drinks as they did not have enough time for that. Then he told us a story which is worth repeating.

A priest in County Cork was giving a mission once and, like all Irishmen, he would have taken a wee dram occasionally. He had instructed the congregation that he did not have time to accept cups of tea and would they please not offer them. That evening he was out doing his rounds and the weather was dreadful, with freezing wind and rain lashing down. The housewives couldn't help offering something hot and the first one he visited said, "Oh, Father, you must be frozen, have a nice cup of hot tea."

"No tea," said the priest and proceeded to do what he had to do.

The second house he visited the lady offered him hot chocolate.

"No chocolate," he said firmly.

On the third visit the sympathetic lady welcomed him with, "Father, you must be frozen. Will you have a glass of whiskey and water?"

"No water," he said.

Whiskey was the drink of choice but most people could not afford it. When young men and women wanted to celebrate they would go to a potin (pronounced potchin) maker who always had a few bottles ready for sale. They kept it well hidden but, if they knew you were coming, it would usually be in the thatch. The police were always on the lookout for distillers and fines were heavy and even jail sentences were severe, so a lot of energy went into evading police and many original hideouts were invented.

Shamey and I were one day in Hughes' moss, just playing, I think, when we noticed a string running along the ground into a well. We pulled it and it was attached to a copper worm which was part of the still. The worm was a copper pipe rolled into concentric circles, through which the steaming alcohol passes and condenses.

We had an idea what it was so we let it drop back again into the well and covered up the string. We never mentioned it again – we were learning fast not to talk.

A new sergeant, Coogan, I think, came to the barracks in Coalisland, determined to stop the illicit distillations. Previously, sometimes the potin men would hide their potin in someone else's haystack or turf stack. Then when the police realised that they hadn't got the bootlegger they would be very frustrated, indeed.

A new law was made that if the potin was discovered on one's land, then that person was guilty. This was very unfair and caused a lot of ill feeling between the police and the people, as a man would be sent to prison who did not know anything about the potin. After that, the distillers discontinued the practice but it was always a running battle with the police, finding a safe hiding place for the product. The smoke from the distilling fires was always a giveaway but as people would come down to work their turf they would sometimes light fires in the moss to make tea and that lessened the suspicion a trail of smoke would make.

Potin is still made to this day and some people would still tell you where you can get a good drop. One man kept his wash in a creamery can, along with those for his milk. The cans were laid out for the creamery man to collect each morning to take to Cookstown creamery. There were about six or eight cans, but he had forgotten to move the potin can the night before and, when he awoke in the morning, the creamery lorry had gone. He hastily dressed and drove to Cookstown, which was some miles away, and he was relieved to see his lorry still in the queue about third from the front. The faulty can was extracted and all was well. I've often wondered how the creamery would have explained hundreds of gallons of alcoholic milk.

As well as the missionary priests, religion of a different hue played a part in our lives. As the days of summer lengthened and school holidays beckoned, the sound of the Lambeg drums could be heard each evening coming from the Inn Corner just across the river. The practising would commence probably in June, in preparation for the Orange men's marching season, and the sound would echo across the countryside and could be heard for miles.

The Orange marches which take place around twelfth July, to celebrate the victory of Protestant King Billy over the Catholic King James at the Battle of the Boyne, are a paradox because King Billy was an ally of the Pope and the Battle of the Boyne had nothing to do with religion. King Billy brought with him a papal blessing and a banner proclaiming the support of the Pope. The Pope welcomed the victory of King Billy and a pontifical high mass was celebrated in Rome in thanksgiving.

The Pope, who was a temporal prince in Italy as well as spiritual, and King Billy were united in opposition to Catholic Louis XIV of France, who had occupied part of Holland and northern Spain and was an ally of King James. So the poor old Pope has taken a bashing every July from the Orange men when he was really a friend on their side and probably contributed men and money to the defeat of King James. (This can all be confirmed on the internet.)

The Lambeg drums were not ordinary drums, but huge drums that measured about four or five feet in diameter. It took a well-built strong man to beat them and great pride was taken in the execution of this task.

The straps of the drum were placed around the drummer's shoulders when the drum was lifted up, just like the big drum in the marching band. The drummer beat both sides of the drum with two sticks and the noise it made was deafening if you were near.

I remember being there when they marched down Thomas Street in Portadown, which was quite a narrow street and the sound was indeed loud. I imagine the drummer's ears had a short shelf life because I had to back off pretty quickly. As the drummer moved at a snail's pace along the street, three or four men, whom I presumed to be relief drummers, walked backwards about one or two yards in front of him and seemed to be listening intently to the drum beats. All these men were of stocky build and would need a lot of strength to carry this heavy piece of equipment and beat a very fast drum roll, as well.

It was fascinating to watch. They were very skilled and dedicated to the job in hand, even though the real purpose was to scare the life out of the Catholics. Listening to the drums on a summer evening as we went about our work became quite hypnotic in the end.

On twelfth July the marching bands set out for their different venues, all dressed up in their finery. A lot of drinking would be done, of course, and then they would go to the field set aside for the speeches which would be given, mostly, by the politicians. And the theme for day was a repeat of every other day over the years, which was "Down with the Catholics". A politician who could think up a good bigoted, memorable phrase was well on the way to being elected.

The method was used to create a siege mentality among the proletariat and make them think the Catholics were going to take over if they didn't turn out and vote. This scenario was pure fantasy, as the Catholics could never have a majority under the gerrymandered rules of the time. Anyway, the politicians whipped the people into a frenzy and they duly delivered them their majority. I remember the first time I was able to read the newspaper, apart from Curly Wee cartoons, I was amazed to read phrases like "A Protestant parliament for a Protestant people" coming from the minister of home affairs.

Of course, when a politician became an MP or a minister, he had to get on with the business of governing the country and all that hype was forgotten. It all seems very familiar.

My mother, who came from a more mixed Protestant and Catholic area, said everyone got on very well until election time. I suppose this was because we were all cut from the same cloth, as it were, as I remember reading a history of the British Isles by Trevellyn and discovered that in the very early times Ireland had been invaded from the south by a tribe called the Scots who settled there and also invaded Scotland, hence the name Scotland.

Arthur's mother, Teresa, in the garden

So when my mother was a young girl during election times, her Protestant friends would be embarrassed by the bigotry of their politicians when they met their Catholic neighbours on the road and would stare at the ground rather than meet their eyes. The elections were like measles, which caused a high temperature and were no good to anyone, except the politicians who were obviously the virus.

Another annual summer event was when Eileen's employers went off on holiday and one year she arrived home, not with Alsatians, but with a little child called Robert, the son and heir of Captain Carson and his wife. Robert was about three years old, I suppose, and we soon got used to his presence. Eileen was Nanny, Peter was Nanny's Daddy and Jim Joe was Uncle Jim.

At the beginning, the school children would shout probably rude things at him as they passed, but Nanny told him they were just naughty boys and that's the term he used dismissively when they were going past.

Of course, in a week or two Robert became part of Hughes' household and was accepted, just like the donkey called Daisy, which also arrived and was installed in the front garden, presumably for Robert to ride.

We presumed wrong, however, because Daisy was in foal and one day the most beautiful little foal called Rosemarie appeared in the garden and mother and daughter became an attraction for passersby to admire.

I loved donkeys and tried to ride Daisy, but she just kicked up her heels and I went flying over her head.

When I was very young I had a craze about these pretty animals. I wanted a donkey and was told I couldn't have one, as children have a new 'want' all the time and they usually pass as something else catches their eye. But my donkey longing persisted and if anyone came to the house I usually asked them if they had a donkey.

Gradually people got to know about me and would tell me stories about their donkeys. Dr. Girvan was a regular visitor with all our children's ailments and he told me he had a blue donkey and he would surely bring it in the car next time he came.

Adults treated children like that then – promising things that would never happen. When the doctor was coming I would be out watching for the blue donkey but, of course, there would be an excuse that he forgot and that he would bring it next time, for sure.

Then I started asking Jim Joe about a donkey and he said he and I would go to the next Moy fair, which was a monthly fair in the town of Moy, and buy a donkey. Nobody told me that this would never happen so, on Moy fair morning, I was up early getting ready, not to go to school but to the fair. As I waited, and there was no sign of Jim Joe, who was going to drive us there, I went down to Hughes' to see if he was ready. He told me his horse had thrown a shoe and he suggested that I go back and ask Daddy if he could borrow Roger's mare.

I think from my father's attitude I gathered that nothing was going to happen. A sad feeling came over me and I went to school instead.

Moy, or the Moy, as it is locally known, held its fair on the first Friday of every month and was once known all over Europe, I've been told, because of its horse fair. People came from places like Greece to purchase horses for the cavalry.

It is a village about four miles away on the Dungannon–Armagh road and straddles the Blackwater river, the main part being in Tyrone. When we were young we often got off school in order to drive the cattle to Moy fair. We would be up bright and early, breakfast eaten, faces shining and hair well combed, and we would set off about eight o'clock, two in front to run ahead and stand in gateways and at corners to steer the cattle in the right direction. Charlie, or Jim Joe, perhaps, would be behind.

We lads did all the running, which was usually only for the first mile or two as the cattle soon got tired, and we plodded the last couple of miles at a steady walk. When we turned up the final three-quarter mile road to Moy, we always dreaded meeting the fat cattle the drovers were taking to the railway station.

These were beef cattle, mostly bullocks, weighing about ten hundredweight each. I think we only had the misfortune to meet them once. They were just like in the western films, about 100 cattle filling the road and the footpaths and back as far as the eye could see. The drovers used their sticks and voices to keep them going fast so they wouldn't have time to get into any gateways. They completely ignored approaching farmers with their half dozen calves or maybe just one cow. If a calf was caught up in the drive it would probably end up at the railway station, so we looked for a house or a field with a wide gate or gates set in from the road and got our cattle into the shelter and then made as much noise as the drovers, and tried to head off the herd as it went past.

The square in the Moy was large. The side that we came into was the cattle side and we found a convenient space that was in a good position and just stood there waiting for buyers. The cattle were now tired and gave no trouble.

The horse fair was on the other side of the square and we liked to make a sale early so that we could go and have a look at the horses – we found this much more exciting. We would watch and listen to the bargaining, which involved lots of spitting on hands, walking away then coming back again, and more slapping of hands.

The seller's assistant would run with the horse on a short rein to show his paces. If they were horse dealers, which they usually were, then the seller would take a piece of ginger that he had been chewing, lift the horse's tail and push it into the horse's bum. The horse would suddenly come alive, probably buck in the air and take off at a lively pace, with the other man hanging on to the rein. Whether this impressed the buyer, I don't know, but if the horse had a dodgy leg, the smarting rectum would take his mind off it at the time as he tried to get away from it. After a lot more spitting and slapping of hands they reached a price and the deal was done – or so we thought, but we hadn't reckoned on the luck penny.

The luck penny would have been mentioned a few times during the negotiations. If, say the horse seller wanted £20 and the buyer was at £18, then he might walk away and come back and say, 'I'll give you nineteen with a pound luck penny.' That was exactly £18 again but the luck penny would have been settled.

The luck penny, really, was a discount given by the seller and was a tradition – the seller must give the buyer a luck penny. Often, they would fight for ages over the luck penny. Maybe the buyer wanted 10 shillings luck but the seller would only offer 5 shillings luck. It would be stalemate until another man might come along who knew them both. He would drag them together and hold both their hands, slapping them together with his solution.

"Give him the 10 shilling luck and then both of you go to the pub and he'll buy you a drink."

The thought of the drink might just settle it as they would both be thirsty and getting ready to finish. Off they would go with their arms around each other and might not emerge for an hour or two. Then they would proceed to tell you that, "This man is the nicest man I have ever met in my life."

If we sold our cattle it was a great relief because there is nothing so depressing as driving them home again. There is no need now to stand in gates and corners because the cattle will walk home at a good pace and we have to keep up with them. They want to get home and they remember the way.

I heard a funny tale about a couple of cattle dealers called Brian and Peter who were brothers in law, married to two pretty sisters. They travelled to all the fairs and bought perhaps a calf or two in the morning and sold it again in the evening at a profit if they could. It was a job that needed experience and judgement if they weren't going to be left with cattle at the end of the day, which had to be driven home and put in a field until another day.

On Friday evenings they would meet in a pub in Coalisland and have a few drinks and discuss things. Brian had no family, but Peter had five little girls. Peter was a more humorous type than Brian and was always laughing and telling a joke. On this particular evening, having settled down and had a couple of drinks, the conversation took a more serious turn, when Brian asked Peter why it was that he and his wife had no success with having a family while Peter's wife seemed to conceive if he smiled at her.

"Well," said Peter, "You and I are in the cattle trade. I know that cows will not produce milk like they should if they are not well cared for and happy. And neither will they have calves if they are neglected and not in good health. The same rules apply to a woman and she must be cared for and cosseted by us males if we are to have a family."

"Oh, I think I know how to take care of my wife without having to listen to you," said Brian.

"Well, maybe you do and maybe you don't," said Peter. "But I'll tell you what to do when you go home tonight and see what you think."

"Okay, fine. Fire away."

"First of all, go up to the chemist now and get some nice perfumed bath salts and talc and present it to your wife. Then tonight or tomorrow night when you both have had a nice long soak, you will sit in your dressing gown or negligee and have a glass of your favourite wine and relax. And then, when she is ready, your wife will get into bed and you will plant a loving kiss on her forehead."

Peter then paused and took a long drink from his glass. Brian waited for him to continue. "Then what?" he said in the end.

"Then," said Peter, "You send for me."

I believe Brian wasn't pleased with the outcome, especially as one or two people had gathered round to listen.

On the road outside our house
two dogs meet at the bend
They stop and sniff intently
at each other's nether end
They take their time and seem
to ponder long on every smell
What it conveys to them
only they alone can tell
It must have significance
what they analyse
Does it tell them much more
than we can realise?
Could it be that each sniff
is like a urine test
If that is so, their analysis
is surely of the best.
Job done they scrape the ground
and then they start to play
No need for files or notes,
the facts are stored away
Will these facts be used
for instinctive solutions
Or do they become part
of canine evolution?

CHAPTER EIGHT

Each year tinkers would arrive in the area and stop for a week or a fortnight just over the high bridge on a quiet road that had no traffic. There were very wide grass verges along this road, so they parked their caravans or maybe just one or two tents on the grass verges, and during the day they would sit there, tap tapping away making tin cans, large and small, half pint and one pint tins, jinny lamps, which were always made of tin, and many other kitchen utensils.

Their wives or their children would go around the houses selling these goods and they were very good and didn't leak. We'd often stand and watch them for a while as we passed by – it was fascinating seeing how deftly they cut and shaped the objects and then gently tap tapped around the edges until it was sealed. They were very skilled.

Then as suddenly as they had arrived, the tinkers would be gone and the grass would be littered with little pieces of tin.

Everything had its season. In the country we didn't have the parks and swings and amenities that children had in the towns, but we had seasons of country pursuits. In spring it was birds' nests. After school we went hunting for birds' nests: along the hedgerows for blackbirds and thrushes, under the thatch for sparrows and starlings, among the heather for larks, which were difficult to find and we mostly stumbled on them by chance, as they laid their eggs on the ground and were well camouflaged.

The first wren's nest I found impressed me very much. It was so well constructed. It was completely round with a tiny hole just big enough to insert one finger. It was very soft and made of little feathers, hairs and moss, I think. We had to learn not to touch the nests and not visit them often, otherwise the bird would forsake it and build another one elsewhere.

The blackbird's nest was made of hay, straw and grass, all coiled around and around, and the thrush's was plastered inside with dried clay just like hard wall. On the ground we might find a curlew's nest or a peewit or lapwing. I remember bringing tea down to Charlie, who was cutting rushes in the bog, and there was a nest of young curlews, just hatched, and running around all over the place. They were smaller than day old chicks but resembled tiny turkeys covered with black spots on an orange background. That's how I remember them.

The Brilla was full or corncrakes. My brother Shamey and I would chase them through the meadows and they would lead us a merry dance. We'd hear them croaking right beside us, very loud, and would dash over there but, of course, they wouldn't be there but would suddenly crake again much further away.

We could find their little runs in the tall meadow grass. Of course, we wanted to find their nests, but we never did. I think they were probably deliberately coming close, calling to us and drawing us away as we were getting too close – the same tactics as those employed by the larks, pretending their wings were broken. We rarely saw a corncrake, as they kept under cover, but we heard them all right. At night they set up such a din, we could hear them in our house.

One night my father came home and said, "Come out and listen to this." It was a very still summer night and we all went out onto the street to listen. It was like a massive orchestra of corncrakes coming from all directions.

Some nights it would be the frogs coming from what was once a tributary of the Blackwater River, now turned into a swamp containing thousands of frogs, and the noise they made travelled for miles on a still night.

Rats were a great threat around the farm. We didn't like mice but we hated rats. Every dog and every man hated rats. One rat could destroy more in a barn than a dozen mice because, where the mice would make a small hole in the base of a sack, a rat would rip it apart from top to bottom, and a ten stone sack of flour, or a two hundredweight bag of cow meal would be destroyed.

We had a Wheaten Terrier dog called Jack and he had a brain and could think, as I found out. The street in front of our house was almost twenty metres long, running downhill. Pipes were laid from a sort of well at the top side, running under the street until it emerged at the hayshed about thirty metres away, where the water poured out and ran down the hill.

There was a rat which I think was attracted to the hens' food in the top garden and Jack had chased it once or twice. But it jumped into the ditch and disappeared into the water pipe under the street and reappeared in safety, way down the hill. Then one evening I heard Jack after the rat and ran up in time to see the rat and Jack drop into the ditch. The rat was making for the escape tunnel and disappeared down the pipe but, instead of Jack sticking his head into the pipe as he had done before, he took off down the street with me at his heels. He flung himself on top of the pipe exit and in seconds out came the rat and wham! that was the end. Dogs have instinct but it took a reasoning brain to work that one out.

Of course, if I told anyone that at the time, no one would really believe it because we all loved to tell a yarn and make it better than it was. So, apart from my family, I told no one.

Another dog which I must mention in despatches is Sport. He was a black and white collie with a few greenish spots as well. When the threshing machine came it was usually a big date for boys and their dogs, for we all knew that underneath those hay ricks the rats would have nested and they all had to be killed. Not one could be left because it would breed and propagate dozens of rats.

As we got almost down to the bottom rows of sheaves which, underneath had dry branches and leaves and rats' nests, usually there were lots of boys' dogs around the rick waiting. But I think there was another threshing going on somewhere and we had only our Sport.

Our rick had been placed by someone with foresight about ten to fifteen paces from the ditch, which was just full of stinking black muck. We knew they would soon make a run for it and, suddenly, rats came out in a burst and headed for the ditch. Sport was amongst them in a flash and seemed to kill them instantly and go for another. He killed six before they reached the ditch but they were close then when we saw the seventh. We roared at Sport but he was already in the air and he threw himself on the rat as it went into the ditch. They both disappeared into the thick black muck.

"He missed it," somebody said. "It's gone."

'"Well, it was impossible," I said.

Sport started to crawl back up the bank. He was just a thick mass of black sticky slime. We couldn't see the shape of him; we could only guess where his head was. We got a piece of straw and we wiped what seemed to be his head and cleared his eyes and then his face and there, still in his mouth, was the rat which he deposited on the grass. Job done.

We also had a big grey tom cat that looked just like a tiger cub. It was very useful as it kept mice and rats at bay. My father kept it in the barn loft at night among the bags of cattle feed and nothing dared come in while the cat was in charge. Then one day it committed a great sin of killing a chicken.

The hens and their chicks just wandered around the yard and the fields and were very vulnerable, but the cat had seemed to know that they were to be left alone. Once a cat takes a young chick it would take them all until none were left. You either killed the cat or got rid of it. But who would take it? Not a farmer.

The driver of the lorry that delivered our cattle feed from the wholesaler in Dungannon was having a cup of tea in the house when my mother happened to mention the cat.

"Well," he said, "we're having a lot of trouble with rats in the warehouse and if it's as good as you say I'll take it with me."

So he put the cat in a sack and put it in the lorry. The next time he came he said the cat had settled in well and had cleared the rats. He saw it walking along the rafters in the roof hunting sometimes. Everybody fed it and made a fuss of it.

For a while we enquired about Tom, but as the weeks passed we forgot about him. Dungannon is about seven miles from our house and we didn't expect to see him again until one morning, about six months after we had given him away, he strolled into the byre at milking time and joined the other cats waiting for a drink of milk. We stared in disbelief and ran into the house to tell the news. Everyone came to see and couldn't believe their eyes. It was like seeing an apparition after all this time.

My mother was in a quandary. It was autumn and there were no chicks about until the spring. So she allowed him back into his usual haunts in the barn loft. When the lorry man next arrived he said the cat had disappeared about a month ago and they thought he may have been killed by a car on the main road outside. When he suggested he take him again my mother told him to rub the cat's feet with butter which he said he would do.

He later reported that the cat had settled down again and this time he didn't come back. But one morning a white cat appeared at our hearth when we were getting ready for school. I was putting on my boots by the side of the fire and there it was, almost creamy coloured, sitting washing its face in front of the fire. Of course, we were all excited about the cat. No one had seen it come in and it seemed quite at home. From that time we began to have a lot of good luck and we put it all down to the cat. My sister Elizabeth won a ton of coal in a raffle, I won a pair of short trousers for a ha'penny in a raffle at school. Someone else won the top money prize in the parish raffle and so on. Then the cat disappeared again and the winning streak ended. Of course, we all said it was a magic cat.

Summer is a busy time on a farm, but it had its compensations as meal times, when working in the meadows, were very special, especially for young people who were always hungry. About midday we would start glancing up towards the house which was just visible searching for someone coming with the food. Eventually someone would arrive carrying a big can of tea and a basket of boiled eggs and soda bread, among other things.

We usually sat along the river bank on the hay where we could look at the little waves and ripples and watch the moorhens and ducks go drifting by. Everyone would be famished and the boiled eggs and freshly made butter and soda bread were delicious.

Grasshoppers were a nuisance as there seemed to be hundreds of them around, hopping on the bread and everything. We just flicked them off and carried on. Afterwards, when most of the men lit their cigarettes, we'd just sit and rest for a while. I remember once we had a young man called Mick McCann who was a beautiful singer. My sister, Mary, asked Mick to sing and he didn't need to be asked twice. He sang a hit song at the time, it was called "Arm in Arm Together" and it was beautiful. Mick became very popular as a guest artist around the dance halls in the parish.

Then it was everybody back to work until evening, when swallows and swifts would start flying over the meadows in their hundreds looking for their evening meals of insects. When we saw them we knew we would soon be going home. It would be a weary bunch of young legs that plodded the mile home and everyone slept soundly that night.

If there was school next morning my mother would have difficulty getting us up and ready. I'm sure that morning we would all be late and it depended on the mood of the Mistress whether we got caned or not. Elizabeth said she would always use the cane if she was wearing her brown shoes. I don't know how accurate that was.

Halfway to school we always met Jinny, an old lady coming from the school pump with a bucket of water. We would ask Jinny what time it was and she would always say nine o'clock. We always hoped she would say five to nine, but she never did.

Autumn was blackberry season and gathering these fruits was a way of making money. Every afternoon, after school, we would all be out blackberrying. There were lots of brambles about the hedges but there were many pickers and we would often go into fields and find that someone had been there before us. But on good days we would find an abundance and quickly fill our cans. There was a man called Mr. Carberry who called each week. He would hang the can of fruit on his hand held scales and give us about a shilling or whatever it was worth. But first, if he saw the juice at the top of the can, he would pour it off onto the road because pouring water onto the blackberries was a great way to increase the weight.

I remember coming past a house once after Mr. Carberry had been there and the road was a beautiful pink where he had poured what must have been about a gallon of juice and it had run down the brae making it all look like fairyland.

There was one lady who was the nearest to a professional picker in the district. She would be out at dawn every day except Sunday and she was called Ally. If Ally had been there before you there would be nothing left.

The season lasted about two months and like everything else it came to an end. Sometimes, when a gang of us came upon Ally, we used to shout, "Ally, Ally, Ally," very fast in unison. She would look up and shout, "What are you Allying about? Does Ally owe you anything?"

She lived with her sister, Mary, who was adept at reading tea leaves. If Mary came into anyone's house it wouldn't be long until a cup of tea was in her hand. One day she was in the shop and Elizabeth asked her to read her cup. Among other things she said that there was going to be an accident outside, and a few minutes later a boy called Tom McMahon was hit on the face with a stick and was brought in bleeding. This enhanced Mary's reputation enormously.

People made a living as best they could. The poor families were kept alive and one way or another got enough to eat. Many of the men worked for the peat company. The reclaimed bog around where we lived was called the moss and was dry except for parts where the turf had been extracted every year until it was below the water table. A very large portion of it belonged the peat company. William Robert Abraham was its manager and the men who cut the turf for Abraham, as he was commonly referred to, were on piece work and were paid by the chain which was twenty-two yards long (20.12 metres).

If the turf was cut downwards, across the grain of vegetation that it once was, then it was called cutting turf and a special two-sided spade was used, and each turf was thrown to a capper who caught it and placed it back in a row to dry.

The method used in the peat moss was called breasting turf. This was cutting horizontally with the grain and placing the turf on its side, one on top of the other about four deep.

Only one man was required for this but it was a hard job because the breaster had to bend down like he was using a shovel and then lift the heavy wet turf up to the bank. I don't know how much he was paid per chain, but I can imagine it wasn't enough.

The turf then had to be dried and that was achieved by first putting them criss-cross on top of each other so that the air could circulate through them and eventually they were put into stacks on the ramparts until lorries would come and take them away.

The stacks looked like little houses, the turf being the bricks and the sides were sloped in to meet at the top so that the rain would fall off the turf and keep the inside dry.

These stacks were a great temptation to local people who could walk into that great plane of turf at night if they were short and get a sack full. Abraham was always complaining about it to anyone who would listen and one day he was holding forth to one of the turf cutters who said to him, "I blame the Fridayers."

"Who are they?" said Abraham.

"Oh, sure you wouldn't know, being of the other kind," he said, meaning Protestant. "They're the people who do the nine Fridays, that is they go to mass and holy communion on the first Friday of every month for nine consecutive Fridays. Holy Joes, that's what they are."

"Ah," said Abraham.

A few days later, he was having a chat to someone standing on the rampart. The two of them lit their fags and Abraham walked over to lean against a stack of turf and when he did he fell right into it, as the turf had been stolen from the inside of the stack and the wall replaced. His companion got the turf off him and pulled him out and the first words Abraham said were, "To hell with the Fridayers."

The peat moss may not have paid much but it kept a lot of families alive. Also, after a certain period, these men would have enough insurance stamps on their cards and be able to draw the dole or the buroo as it was called locally.

While drawing the buroo, people weren't averse to doing a job for the local farmers at busy times like bringing in the hay. One promising day my father rounded up a few men for the Brilla as the weather forecast was good, or maybe my father's big toe might have warned him that he had but a day to finish the meadow. Usually, the meadows were well hidden from prying eyes but we had one meadow that came very near to the main road and that's where we were on this day.

The buroo men would be on the lookout for one or two men about whom they had their suspicions, having been given a tip-off from a jealous neighbour, perhaps, and they would slowly cruise around the roads, hoping to catch them red-handed. They usually carried binoculars and because of this some men adopted disguises.

I heard from my nephew Colm of a man who met another man on the road one morning, who was sporting a red beard and wore dark glasses. He didn't know who this bearded man was, but there was something about him that seemed familiar. When he told his wife she said, "Och, do you not know your own son? He's away to his work."

When we were working in the meadow near the road one man called John was very wary as he raked the hay into a pile and his eye would stray to the road, looking for a car which might contain the buroo man. There were only one or two regular cars which used the road and they were well known. I was right beside him and I think he had attracted my attention with his furtive glances and talk of mysterious buroo men. He suddenly threw himself on the ground and the man beside him threw a forkful of hay on top of him. John lay there for a few minutes until the car had passed out of sight and then he was prodded and the all clear was announced.

I remember once coming from school with a boy called Paddy who said to me, "I wish I was eighteen, Arthur, and I could go on the buroo, like our John." What ambition, between the buroo and the peat moss.

Another source of income was from flax. Quite a lot of flax was grown in the district and there was a scutching mill, as well, quite near. When the flax was ready to be harvested it was still green and would be pulled out by the roots. Usually a gang of men would pull a field in a day or two. It would be tied in sheaves like oats or barley or wheat, and finally it was taken to the flax hole to be steeped, that is soaked in water for about two weeks, I think. I'm not sure because we didn't grow flax.

The canal, at one point, ran along the Coalisland road, and between the canal and the road, flax holes had been opened and were all ready full of water from the canal. The flax holes were about eight or nine feet wide and about thirty feet long – I'm guessing now. The flax sheaves were put on their ends, bottom end up, and packed in rows tight against each other. The sods would be cut from the surrounding area and placed on the flax to push them down and keep them there. Now, one could walk over them, if necessary.

While the flax was retting – that was the name given to it – the smell of stagnant water would begin to permeate the countryside, but that was only a foretaste of what was to come. When it was thoroughly retted, which was when the outside layer of the stalk fell away from the centre (the linen fibre), a brave man was needed to continue the process. The sods were removed and replaced on the land and the brave man appeared with nothing on but an old pair of trousers and shoes. He had to get in there up to the waist in the stagnant pool and lift the sheaves out to be stacked and dried and taken to the scutching mill to be scutched: separating the fibre from the rest.

Coalisland had its own linen mills and that is where it eventually ended. Afterwards the owner would wait for his cheque to arrive depending on the yield.

Incidentally, the country would be stinking during this time, but we got used to it. The smell always reminds me of when I learned to swim or, rather, when I got my feet up off the bottom. There was a little river called the Tarn which ran parallel to the canal down to the Blackwater river. We who lived down in Derrytresk, that is young chaps, would go to bathe in the Tarn at a place called Proghy. It was only waist deep and the Tarn was fast flowing and always clean. Every Sunday I tried to swim but I could only ever get one foot off the bottom. I think I had a fear of drowning.

One Sunday I came home and decided I would go the next day by myself and sort out this problem. It had been raining all night but I went anyway and when I got to the Tarn I couldn't believe my eyes as it had overflowed its banks and was careering along like a mill stream. Worse than that, it had washed all the stagnant water out of the Coalisland flax holes and the water smelled very badly but I wasn't deterred. I stripped off, went in and found the water was up to my neck and lifting me off my feet. I turned and went with the flow doing swimming actions and there I was swimming away in what I imagined to be the correct way, at break-neck speed with feet thrashing. After that, I could float and do a very poor breast stroke, but I never became a 'swimmer'. It took me a long time to get rid of the stinking smell, as it clung for weeks and I got a lot of funny looks for a while.

CHAPTER NINE

When I was thirteen I went to the Academy in Dungannon, a Catholic secondary school where an entrance exam was required in order to get a scholarship for two years. I don't believe anyone did not get a scholarship; it was quite simple.

It was seven miles from where I lived so, naturally, I travelled by bicycle and usually got home about four in the afternoon. There were about half a dozen of us who travelled home together and usually we would be larking about racing each other, so I didn't look around much at the countryside. Then one day I caught the glimpse of a dog's tail in the distance across a flat piece of grazing land. It was a few hundred yards away, hidden by rushes but it looked exactly like my dog Nora's tail. When I got home she was at the door wagging her tail and I thought I was mistaken.

When I saw it again in the distance a few weeks later I was intrigued. It was always about the same spot, about three or four miles from our house. When I mentioned it to my mother she said that Nora would be lying asleep in the kitchen and she would suddenly jump up and take off at the same time every day. She said she didn't seem to wake up first but went straight from sleep to motion.

So that's what she did. Each day she came to meet me, not coming near but keeping me in sight, or maybe keeping me in scent. She got home before me and watched at the gate or at the door. I wonder if I was late would she also anticipate that? I wish I could understand the instinct of animals. Someday somebody will and that will be a breakthrough worth waiting for, particularly if we can plant the stem cell in humans.

I started the Academy in 1939, when the war was about to start. It was called the phoney war to begin with, because although all the preparations were going ahead, like the issuing of gas masks and the building of air raid shelters, no fighting was taking place involving the allied forces and the Germans. The British Expeditionary Force and the French were sitting behind the Maginot line facing the German forces, sitting behind the Siegfried line, and not a shot was being fired.

The eight o'clock news each morning would announce, "All quiet on the western front," and it became a bit of a joke until, eventually, one morning on the eight o'clock news again, we heard that Hitler had ignored the Maginot line and just drove his tanks around it, through Belgium and down to Paris. The Allies were eventually driven back and British Expeditionary Force escaped across the channel at Dunkirk.

When the war broke out the radio was everyone's link to the rest of the world. My mother would turn it up in the morning, I think to waken us all up to get ready for school, and I used to lie for a while listening to the progress of the war. When Churchill proclaimed that Britain was fighting for the freedom of small nations, we would all roar with laughter and shout at the radio, "What about this small nation?" And when the British army was forced to withdraw and Mr. Churchill made his "Fight on the beaches" speech, I wrote a two line poem in my exercise book.

> We will fight on the beaches, our great leader said,
> But don't you dare defend yourself if on your land we tread.

Some people were pro German mainly because they didn't understand. They imagined Hitler coming on a white charger and setting us all free. Jim Joe Hughes was very pro German and he and my father had such arguments nearly every night. My father would get very red in the face trying to reason with him. Jim Joe said that under Hitler's socialist regime all land would be divided up in equal shares to everyone and we would all work for the common good. I think he confused Hitler's socialist regime with communism. My mother used to say, "Don't argue with him," but as soon as Jim Joe started the battle would commence again.

Lord Haw Haw was eagerly listened to. He was the German propagandist and we would all gather round the radio in the evening to hear him. All we wanted to hear was a mention of Northern Ireland and when he said something like, "What about the downtrodden people of Northern Ireland?" we thought, "Yes, somebody cares. Somebody out there knows about us." That gave us hope.

I don't think there was any Irish history taught to the Unionist children or, if there was, it was doctored to suit the situation. The English people knew very little Irish history. At the time of the recent troubles, most people hadn't much knowledge of what the fighting was about. In a television programme about Northern Ireland one evening, some Ulster Protestant school children were being asked questions about their history and they all thought that they were the indigenous population and that the Irish were the usurpers.

Just before the war was declared a few people from Coalisland, fearing conscription, hightailed it across the border and joined the Irish army, but also a lot joined the British army. A family near us, called Rush, lost their three sons, Peter, Barney and Patsy. Patsy was my age and I knew him very well.

But the preparations in Dungannon continued. We would hear the air raid sirens practising every day when we were in class and learned to distinguish between the air raid warning and the all clear.

Air raid shelters began to appear all around us, built with reinforced concrete. The first one I noticed was in Church Lane and there was the blackout, of course. Car headlights were covered with a black material with a small hole about two inches by three inches, through which a tiny beam of light shone and was all the driver had.

There wasn't much bombing in Northern Ireland, except in Belfast, which was very heavily bombarded. The most exciting thing that happened for us lads was that a new cinema opened up in Castle Hill. Before that there had only been the Astor in George Street.

On my first day at the Academy, a little chap called Bill McCann from Cookstown told me at lunchtime to come to a shop halfway up Church Street on the other side from Murray Richardson's, the stationer's, where we got a cup of tea and I don't remember what else, but maybe biscuits, but he also told me I could get broken biscuits at half price in Burton's at the corner of Church Street and the Square. Bill was definitely my financial adviser.

The principal, or headmaster, of the Academy was Father McKernon, a larger than life man who amazed us with his eccentricities from the beginning. He taught us Latin and we never knew what to expect when he came into the class. One day he said, "I don't feel like doing anything today so I suggest we all sleep." Everyone had to put their heads on their arms and sleep and if they didn't he would call out their names.

He had his car parked outside the classroom window and some days he would stand their admiring it for a long time with his hands deep in his soutane pockets, and he would carry on a conversation with any of the boys about him, particularly my friend Bill who sat next to me.

"Bill McCann," he would say, "Do you think that's a very posh car?"

"Yes, Father," Bill would naturally reply.

"Who do you think a car like that would belong to?" was the next question.

"You, Father," Bill would say.

"No," he'd reply. "Wouldn't you think it belonged to Chinny Davidson. That's who you would think, isn't it?"

"Yes, Father."

I surmise that Chinny Davidson must have been a rich businessman or entrepreneur, but I had never heard of him before.

Father McKernon also had a parrot in a cage and some days he'd bring it into class. The parrot spoke exactly like him, which was with a nasal twang, and many times we were scared out of our wits by Father McKernon's voice right behind us, as he had a habit of leaving the cage in different places in the garden, perhaps to let the parrot get the sun.

He also had a wire fox terrier called Rory. Often you would hear Father McKernon calling "Rory" only to find it was the parrot speaking.

In front of the door of his residence was a little wood with lots of tall trees and shrubs. When we came in we cycled around it to the bicycle shed. If we were late we might hide in the wood until the second period as that was when Father McKernon did the roll call. But the first morning I tried the wood I got a shock when I heard Father McKernon's voice shouting, "Come out of the bushes; come out of the bushes."

I was just about to do that when the boy who was with me, said, "It's the parrot," and, sure enough it was.

Dungannon parish chapel was just a hundred yards past the Academy, and on Sunday mornings Father McKernon would say one of the masses there. On the morning when the priests' dues were collected, he had his own unique way of extracting money from the congregation. Normally, the priest would walk beside the altar boy who had a tray for collecting the donations and the altar boy would call out the name of the donor, such as, "James O'Brien 5/-," and the priest would repeat it in a loud voice.

Or that was what he was supposed to do, but Father McKernon would pause and say something like, "He could afford more than that," or something similar. Of course, the congregation looked on it as a bit of light relief, except for poor Mr. O'Brien.

So that was our headmaster, with his two assistants Rory and Polly and, of course, his shiny new car.

As the war progressed and food became scarcer, rabbits became very popular as a source of meat. When I realised that I could get one shilling each for a rabbit I bought snares and, under Charlie's instructions, I set them all over the farm and moss. In the mornings I would set off running before school to check my snares and often I was late for school as my snare area got bigger.

Ferrets became very popular, as well. Rabbits were terrified of ferrets as they could go into the burrows after them, so the rabbits had no safe haven. The ferrets were really pets; they would go to sleep in one's coat pocket or anywhere that it was warm and were easily fed and cared for.

When a ferret was taken to a rabbit burrow it would disappear down a hole, and if rabbits were inside they would come flying out, terrified. They would be caught by putting rabbit nets over the holes or shooting or killing with dogs. The nets were the best, of course, but at the beginning we weren't that sophisticated.

Sometimes the ferret might kill a rabbit in the burrow. If it didn't come out again, then we had an idea that that is what happened. When the ferret had had enough to eat he would fall asleep underground, and they are very good sleepers so there isn't any point in waiting.

The first time this happened I was with a boy called Michael who owned the ferret. Michael knew not to wait around and said he would come back the next day when he would meet me at the burrow in the morning. When he came he had a piece of fried bacon tied to a piece of string and he placed it at the entrance to the burrow. Very soon the ferret appeared, blinking in the daylight, and he popped it into his box.

I sold my rabbits to Murphy the Beef man, as we called him, who called every Tuesday evening and more or less twisted my mother's arm until she went out to the van and bought something.

"Come on away over, Mrs. Mac," he would say.

"No, I don't need anything, Mr. Murphy."

"Och, sure you don't know until you've had a look. Come on away over."

In spite of all her protests he won the majority of the battles and my mother would return with at least a pound of sausages. I would be waiting with my rabbits and he would give me a shilling each.

Once a weasel or something had eaten the head off a rabbit but he still gave me 9d for it. I liked my mother to go over to the van because if it was bad weather, or raining hard, Mr. Murphy might not bother opening the van.

"Away with you. I haven't the time," he would say and I'd be left with the rabbits.

If it was wintertime the rabbits would keep for a few days, but in the summer it was more difficult. Then I heard at school from another entrepreneur that Fairburns in Dungannon was paying 1/6d for rabbits. So I put them in a sack and got the bus from Tamnamore corner, three-quarters of a mile away. The return fare was only 4d. When I got off the bus I had another mile to go but I thought it was worth it, and so it was.

One day my sister Mary, who was on her summer holidays from boarding school, had arranged to meet some school friends in Dungannon. She was outside the stationer's shop in Church Street and when she looked down the street she saw me coming towards her.

When she got home she said, "Oh, Mammy, I had such a narrow escape. I was outside Murray Richardson's and when I looked down the street I saw Arthur coming with a sackful of rabbits on his back. I had to rush everybody back into the shop and buy a pen that I didn't need and keep them inside until he was gone."

I went once a week with my rabbits in the wintertime but in the warm summer weather I had to go twice a week. Once I thought my rabbits were fine and I set off on the bus but in a short time I became aware of a smell and on investigating I found that it was the rabbits. Soon the conductor came past me and stopped and looked at me hard.

"What have you got in that bag," he asked.

"Rabbits," I replied.

"Well, you'll have to get off or else throw your rabbits off," he told me.

So, off I got. It was out in the country so I emptied my rabbits out on the roadside. I knew the one it might be as I had taken a chance with it. I threw the rabbit over the hedge and the rest were fine. I got the next bus into Dungannon and all was well.

Even once I started at the Academy I still liked to call into Hughes' after school. As I grew older so did Eileen and, naturally, her boyfriends became more mature. I remember one Sunday afternoon a quite fat solicitor arrived from Dungannon, who seemed to have over-indulged himself with a liquid luncheon. Eileen wasn't at home so Peter took him down to the parlour, gave him a drink and asked my sisters, Mary and Kathleen, who were in the house, to go down to chat to him. Kathleen told us, "Mary chatted away to him about the beauty of the sun shining on the heather until the poor man's eyes started to close. Finally, he gave us money to go and get sweets. He was gone when we came back."

Another time, Mary or Kathleen had to help Eileen out when she had double dated, by getting one man out of the window while Eileen held up her unexpected visitor in the hall.

One particular night, Eileen had a date with a taxi man called George, whom Peter knew quite well. George was late and Peter didn't know he was a date. When he appeared Peter gave him what for.

"Holy boots, what time do you call this? She's been waiting for ages."

George just smiled and apologised.

124

It was about this time that the house where Eileen was nanny was visited by a burglar. Eileen was alone with the children babysitting when a man appeared from nowhere and he said, "If you show me where the jewels are kept, I won't harm you."

"I'll give you jewels," said Eileen and she lifted a cut glass tumbler from the sideboard and hit him over the head with it, then called the police. Her photograph appeared in the paper the next day. That was Eileen.

CHAPTER TEN

There were so many characters in our neighbourhood. Nearly everybody developed their own little ways and habits, most of which were amusing and enjoyable.

My cousins, John, Joe, James and Ellen, lived with their mother, Maggie Magennis, my Uncle Peter having died prematurely. Maggie was of the old school and still wore a shawl when going out to town or to church. A few older ladies did still wear shawls and I can also remember Jemmy Campbell, The Hat, sporting a fancy green coat – perhaps, it was called a frock coat – very ornate and gathered at the back with pleats and buttons. It was his Sunday coat and he had a special bowler for Sunday, as well.

Maggie was a shy person who was kind and friendly to talk to, but had an unusual way of telling anything. She didn't like naming people or things, almost as if that was too open and easily understood. I wondered if it was something to do with the British occupation. Maybe she had been told to be careful with names and what she said, just like in war time later when "Don't forget that walls have ears" posters appeared. At any rate it made her very amusing. She would walk to Coalisland and back, carrying her shopping, and that was about three miles away. Then she would tell you, "I got a bit of thing for him, went to him with the hat, them ould dogs." As her eyes were always running, she would be rubbing the corner of each eye alternately with her fingers, right and left, punctuating each phrase.

Frances would translate for me when I told her. She said, "She bought cheap meat for John's dogs, from Tomney the butcher, who always wears a hat, and she is fed up with John's dogs."

She never referred to any of the boys by name, she called them all him or he, and the boys did the same, but I think she referred to her daughter as Ellen. This was very confusing and I never knew to whom any of them was referring. I found that each got impatient and angry if I pressed the point, as if I was just being obtuse, so I learned to settle for an educated guess.

Maggie didn't own a radio but we had one that sat on our window sill. One day she asked me, "What did that old boy in your window say about the weather?"

In later years, when there was only John and James left, my brother Shamey told me that he used to press John when he said him meaning James, to make him say the word James.

Shamey would say, "But who, John, who do you mean?"

And then he would explode with, "James," as if he were having a tooth pulled.

Everybody walked or cycled to the towns, which, as I've mentioned before were three and seven miles away, as we didn't have any public transport until the war started and then things began to happen.

Maybe we weren't worthy of such luxuries, but war changed all that. Soon the countryside was covered with troops training, a new aerodrome was being built along the lough shore and everyone had a job either at the aerodrome or rebuilding in Belfast, which was heavily bombed.

Petty hates had to be forgotten and a bus service began from Derrytresk to Dungannon via Coalisland. Oh, there was some excitement then, even though it only ran one day a week, on Thursday. The old ladies never missed the bus and the tales that followed those trips were good entertainment.

On the first day there was a lady called Jane and when the conductor asked her what ticket she wanted, she said, "There and back."

Still in a good humour, as it was early in the day, and he had no idea what naivety he was going to experience, he said, "Oh, we'll get you there and back all right, but where are you going?"

"I'm going with you, so I am," says Jane.

"To the town, then," he said.

"I am," said Jane.

"Is it Coalisland, then?"

"No, it's not the Island. Sure, I could walk there," said Jane.

"You're going to Dungannon, is that it? That will be 1/3d then."

"No, it's not. I'm not going all the way – just nearly there."

"Where exactly is the stop you're going to?"

"Here as you go in, on the left," said Jane.

"Is it a shop, you're going to?"

"No, it's not," said Jane, with a tolerant smile and wondering at his stupidity. "It's a…" and she looked over her shoulder and lowered her voice. "It's a bank," she whispered.

"It's the Northern Bank – that's where you're going. There's a stop right outside it," said the conductor.

It seems Jane was embarrassed. People kept their affairs very quiet. Even to have a bank account would be a well guarded secret. Somebody might get the idea that you had money and that wouldn't do at all, at all.

She got her ticket and was very subdued for the remainder of the journey. When Jane got off the bus with her travelling companion, she said, "You go and do your business and I'll do mine," and she waited until the coast was clear before entering the hallowed portals of the Northern Bank. To have been a fly on the wall at the counter would have been a treat.

That bus was full up every Thursday and later the service was extended throughout the week.

Dungannon was a good shopping town with shops such as Alexander's drapers and Fred W. Robertson hardware in the Square. My father had accounts in these two shops, as he bought clothes and farming implements from them to retail in his shop.

Across the road was Marshall's Chemist next to Burton's Confectioner and McAleer's Hotel on the corner of Thomas Street, which Eileen had often mentioned in her accounts of her soirees.

At that time, pubs had snugs leading off the street where, if one wanted privacy, there was no need to enter the pub proper. The customer just slipped into the snug and the barman, who was always the soul of discretion, would slide back a panel, take your order and serve you your drink.

I remember my mother and my aunt Maggie went to Dungannon, which is the only time that I can remember they ever did, because they lived a few miles apart, which is a long way if one is walking. They both returned about 4:30 in the afternoon and I noticed that they were a bit flushed and giggly and I discovered that they had slipped into a snug in Scotch Street. It was at the corner of Shamble Lane, which was very convenient because if anyone noticed someone turning into the lane they wouldn't know where they were going, as the snug was only a few paces away and easy to disappear into. So they had a half one or two and came out again feeling all the better for it. At that time it wasn't done for ladies to go into a pub without a chaperone.

At the beginning of the war, I suppose in 1939, a new force was formed called the B Specials, or B-men, as they became known. These were not like the Home Guard to protect us from Hitler, but to quell the anticipated Irish Catholic uprisings, and they were all well armed. They wore different uniforms than the police and, of course, were wholly Protestant, and their chief activity seemed to be harassment of Catholics.

They would stop us when we were coming home from the cinema or from dances at weekends and examine our bicycles. The following month there would be a list of fines imposed. All our names would be listed: no bell 2/6d; defective brake 5/-; no light 5/-; defective tyre 5/-.

This was harassment of a community, as we were informed it didn't happen in the Protestant areas. Five shillings was a lot of money at that time and most of the young people would find it difficult to pay. A lot of the B Specials were just ordinary farmers and labourers who were decent enough and just joined it to supplement their incomes. But, there were also those who loved bullying the Catholics.

One of our own men called Alec, who was a bit of a wag and was also always playing practical jokes, made a speciality of staging hold-ups on dark nights. If we were all coming from a dance or church, on bicycles, of course, Alec would be waiting up ahead with a strong flash lamp and wave us down. He would have his trilby hat turned upside down and would proceed to examine identity cards and check bicycles, until one's eyes got used to the dark and caught on. Then somebody would shout, "It's only Alec," and we would all be relieved that it was.

Sunday night was usually dance night. The AOH hall, or Ancient Order of Hibernian Hall in Derryloughin was our mecca every week. It was built on the moss from timber and zinc and it was well run and provided a meeting place for young folks, which was very necessary. My older sisters, Mary, Kathleen and Elizabeth, would go regularly to the Sunday night dance and I tagged along with them probably from when I was about twelve.

There were quite a few of my friends there as well and we just treated it as if it were a school playground. One night Paddy Hagan, a school friend who lived near me, began to play on the drums for the band and the next night he let me have a go and for a while afterwards we took it in turns each night. I suppose the drummer was glad of the break, but Paddy and I loved it and were learning fast. It was quite simple really, with one foot on the pedal of the big drum going boom, boom, boom, to give the rhythm, and then doing whatever we felt like on the other equipment.

We were learning to dance as well and one lad used to take out a forty year old unmarried woman who attended regularly, and I thought that must the thing to do, so I began dancing with her as well. I'm sure she wasn't a bit pleased to see me coming to ask her to dance, but we didn't know any better and perhaps, if she wasn't getting danced, she would welcome it. We'll never know.

My father would lock the door at midnight. It was a security door and couldn't be opened from the outside. So if we were late and had to get him up he wouldn't be pleased. As the three girls went in ahead of me they each got a cuff around the ear, but when I came in with my head well down behind them, he'd just give me a shove.

When we were older we started going over to Mahery, a village that was situated about two miles from Derryvarn where the river joined Lough Neagh. Mahery was on the Armagh side of the river and there was a ferry big enough to take horses and carts and cars across. If the ferry was on the Tyrone side, all one had to do was pull on the rope to the other side and Mahery Hotel was about 200 yards further up the road. It was quite a pretty place: the lake extending outwards with Coney Island and Scady Island in the distance, and the river flowing into it to the left. Mahery's main attraction to young people was the dance that was held there every Sunday night in the hotel. There would also be dinner dances and it was very popular with all classes.

A big attraction was a bar upstairs, which was supposed to be closed on Sundays, but it did a good trade in spite of that. The dance hall walls were lined with mirrors and on the mirrors was chalked "No jitter bugging allowed". That didn't stop the jitter buggers, because the Yanks were stationed in the vicinity and they were a joy to watch, throwing the girls between their legs and then over their heads.

The Yanks came up from Ardbo aerodrome, and other places in Tyrone. They parked their jeeps along the road on the Tyrone side and would go across on the ferry.

They were very popular with girls and also the pubs, as they had lots of money and weren't afraid to spend it.

One night, two Yanks came strolling up from the ferry, shining, as usual, in their beautiful uniforms, and they asked the yardman, "Say, buddy, can you get us a couple of bottles of whiskey?"

"Sure," the man said.

"How much is that?" said the Yank, putting his hand into his pocket.

"Ten bob," said the yardman.

"Gee, what's that then, bud?" asked the Yank.

"Just a pound," said the yardman, doubling the price.

"Okay, a pound it is, bud," said the Yank, but they didn't mind.

Another incident I witnessed was when a Yank walked his girl, whom he had probably met at the dance, down to the ferry. They said their farewells and he waited and waved to her as she boarded. Then he turned and strolled back to the dance. We were standing nearby and happened to be watching. He put his hand into his pocket and then he stopped and started to search his pockets; his wallet was gone.

"Gee I've been robbed," he said.

He ran back to the river, dived in and streaked across the river with a beautiful fast crawl. We watched as he ran up the road, got his wallet from the girl and walked back to the ferry. As it was a warm night and he was young and fit, I don't suppose it did him any harm.

A friend told me of another incident at the ferry. The ferry had wooden rails along each side and people would lean on them as they crossed, looking out at the waves and relaxing. But there was one spot where there was a break in the rails and there was a chain across for safety.

On this particular night the chain hadn't been connected and there was a man there called Patrick who was talking to two girls just at the break in the rails. He had what was known as a posh accent for the area, and after he made some witty remark to the girls he put his hand behind him to lean on the rail but, alas, the rail wasn't there and he fell back into the river. My friend said he disappeared for a few seconds and he thought, "I'll find out now if his accent is genuine."

When his head appeared above the water, he had drifted away from the boat and as he trod water he shouted, "Someone throw me a rope," with the accent still intact.

We did enjoy those nights at Mahery Hotel. People came from miles around: from Portadown, Dungannon and local towns. It was unique to the area.

CHAPTER ELEVEN

I've mentioned that Peter Hughes and his son Jim Joe were completely different characters, but time didn't heal their differences, it just exacerbated them. I think it was mostly Jim Joe's fault, as he didn't seem to be able to tolerate Peter at all. Jim Joe was like the freemasons – everything on the level and on the square – while Peter was more of an artist and hadn't much time for levels or squares. He preferred growing flowers, weaving baskets and making little summer houses from woven osier rods.

Our houses were within a hundred to two hundred yards of each other, with our farms fanning out radially from each one, and with nothing between us but fields. With practically dead stillness all around we could hear a raised voice like it was beside us. Mary Donaghy, for instance, bringing in the cows sounded so clear it was like she was standing beside us.

"Come on, you old bugger," she would shout, and you could imagine her poking it with a stick.

There was no privacy. Jim Joe and Peter both had high carrying voices and when they were shouting there was nothing left to the imagination.

Shamey told me that one morning when he was going to school, which was about a mile away, he listened to them all the way until he closed the school door. The row could start from anything and one massive row started when Peter let the tea boil over.

Jim Joe had a bull calf that he thought a lot of and he decided not to have it doctored with the rest, as he thought it would make sire material. When it reached a certain age it had to be passed by the ministry inspector, but it failed. I remember it well and I didn't like it myself, although I wasn't an expert. An order was given to have the bull castrated, which Jim Joe refused to do. He finished up in the law court and was fined, but he refused to pay and was sent to jail where he spent a few days, until Eileen paid his fine and had the bull castrated.

Another time he killed a sow pig – a sow pig was one which had had one litter. At that time they were bought by the ministry, so Jim Joe brought the pigs to the abattoir to have them graded according to quality. The heads were all cut off the pigs and they were labelled and hung up as they were graded.

When Jim Joe got his docket he got a grade two, which he refused to accept. The official assured him that his pig had had a litter and was, therefore, a sow pig, grade two. Jim Joe wanted to see his pig and when he was shown it, he said, "That's not my pig."

"Why?" said the vet.

"Because my pig had a head," he said.

I understand that the row lasted all day, because Jim Joe never gave in and he says he got his grade one in the end.

He was relating this episode in our house one night to Father Regan, our curate. When he had finished, Father Regan said, "Jim Joe, would that not bother your conscience?"

"No, Father, I'll never trouble you in the confessional with that one," he said.

So, Peter and Jim Joe continued to row and became the talk of the countryside and, when Eileen came home she got involved, as well.

Jim Joe had built himself a large boiling house with a high brick fireplace where he could boil a huge pot of spuds and other foods for his pigs, of which he had quite a lot. He moved his bed in there and started to sleep there and this quietened things for a while, but not for long.

Left to right: Arthur, 16, Jim Joe Hughes, and Arthur's cousin James Magennis

Eileen's nursing job had finished by then and she came home permanently and did some casual local nursing. She developed severe migraine attacks and took to her bed for days at a time. The rows continued between Jim Joe and Peter and now Eileen, as well.

One morning Jim Joe threw a bucket of water over Kate, his mother, in bed. That night my father decided to discuss the order of the bath with Jim Joe but he only gave him a funny look and decided not to take the bait. Eventually, Peter signed the farm over to Eileen and Jim Joe was disinherited.

Eileen then married a man called George who, of course, had the necessary car, and Jim Joe began lodging with different neighbours and acquaintances. I remember coming home from college at Halloween break to find that Jim Joe was asleep right in the middle of the bed I was going to share with Shamey. Shamey just got into the bed and gave him a shove and said, "Lie over to the stock, boy." Then I got in and we all slept well.

After Eileen married George and they had returned from their honeymoon, she invited all the local children to another party. My mother didn't tell us what to do, so I am now ashamed to say, Elizabeth and I arrived with "our two hands the one length". That was a phrase of my mother's and meant we had brought nothing. But neither did anyone else, with one exception. Eileen was friends with a family from Tamnamore called Cranson. She invited Sue and Melvyn, for that was their names, to the party. I seem to recall that they were a lot older than the rest of us.

During the festivities Eileen asked us who was going to be the first to propose a toast to the bride and groom. The only toast I knew was toasted bread so I was completely in the dark. Then Sue and Melvyn Cranson stood up and said a little rhyme, which started, "We wish you health, we wish you wealth." Well, we were all struck dumb until Eileen said, "Who's next?"

And then we looked at each other, like children will do, for inspiration. Eileen said to the boy nearest, called Joey, "Come Joey, stand and wish health to the bride and groom." Joey did so and Eileen said, "Now, each one can take it in turn."

So each one stood up and said, "Health to the bride and groom," but the pace got faster and faster, until we were jumping up and mumbling, and gradually only half standing up and still mumbling, and in the end just bobbing up until there was chaos.

Eileen wasn't perturbed and thanked us very much for our kind wishes – a lady to the last. Elizabeth was imitating the toast for weeks afterwards and kept us all stitches.

When the spring came, the crops had to be planted and ploughing had to begin, but we didn't have a ploughman. Shamey was just twelve years old at the time and Jim Joe was not quite left and not quite at home, so he took one of his little breaks and disappeared for a time, not reckoning on Shamey being able to do anything about it.

Shamey went down to his neighbour Tom Gartland, with whom we were then joined for the ploughing and suggested that they have a go at the tillage.

"Can you set the sock?" asked Tom.

"Certainly," said Shamey.

"Right, I'll bring the horse up in the morning," Tom replied.

I must tell you that Shamey, from when he was a toddler, had a craze about horses and harnesses. He would spend all his spare time harnessing the wheelbarrow, putting in every buckle and clip, and putting the leather reins through all the little keepers etc. and it was all perfect. Then he might sit and drive for a while but soon it would be all undone again and again.

At first, he had been content with the working harness, which was well worn and he couldn't do any harm. But he now wanted the best harness with the gleaming silver and adornments shining in the sun. These were kept in the outside loft, hanging on pegs on the wall. They were all best black leather kept pliant with harness oil and bright silver polish. I think my father liked to see Jim turned out well in the trap, although he didn't have the time to drive around now.

Well, he thought the best harness was safe from Shamey but he was wrong. Shamey climbed up the steps to the loft one Sunday afternoon, opened the back door that was never opened, dragged the harness off the wall and pushed them out onto the dung hill underneath.

He had it all worked out because although it was about an eight foot drop onto the dung hill, it was horse manure which is comparatively dry and clean and would brush off fairly well. He would then drag them into the large hay shed and proceed to harness the wheelbarrow as before. Eventually, I believe they had to let him have his way because that is what he lived for at that time when he was a little boy.

That story reminds me of a joke. A man's mother-in-law, who was a bit posh, arrived at lunchtime.

"What are you doing today, John?" she asked him conversationally.

"Oh, I'm just putting a few loads of dung on the top field," he said.

Afterwards, she spoke to her daughter about it.

"Don't you think you should ask John to say manure?" she said.

"Oh, for heaven's sake, mother, I've only recently got him to say dung."

So, to continue with the ploughing story, Tom Gartland brought up his horse, and Shamey set the plough. They took the two horses and hitched them up and Shamey ploughed his first field at the age of twelve.

A few days later, while he was ploughing another field, Jim Joe appeared on the road, stepped in and took over again.

A few years later, Jim Joe, who was sleeping in the boiling house at night, went missing for a few days and no one knew where he was. People began to get worried and eventually Shamey and Johnny Taggart went to Hughes' to investigate. Shamey lifted Johnny up to the window at night and he saw Jim Joe lying dead in the bed. The post mortem revealed that he had a brain tumour which had killed him, but also accounted for his quirky personality.

Do you remember that day
when making the hay
Where the Blackwater river flows
down to Lough Neagh
You came down the rampart
bringing the tay
And I said, Pretty lady,
are you going to stay?

No, no, I must go
I've got seams to sew
Bread to be baked,
places to go.
So I said in a fright,
will you meet me tonight,
And we'll go for a walk
in the evening light

So that's what we did
in the cool of the day
While the low flying swifts
were skimming the hay
We stood on the bank
of the broad rippling river
And said we'd be true
forever and ever

CHAPTER TWELVE

I didn't like school and I didn't like the Academy but I liked working on the farm at this time and I thought that's where my future lay. So I wouldn't go back to the Academy after the summer break and continued working on the farm.

When I was about fifteen I was sent down to a meadow to open it for the mowing machine. This meant that with a scythe I would cut the grass in the four corners of the meadow and at the entrance about six yards along each side, thirty-six square yards at each corner. This allowed the horses and the mowing machine to enter without flattening all the grass so there was no loss of good hay.

It was a very hot day and it would have taken me about one and a half hours to complete. Tired and hot, I lay down on my back on the cut grass in the far corner when I had finished for a few minutes, as I thought, to wait for Jim Joe and the machine to arrive. I was awakened by a commotion of shouting and clanking machinery. When I opened my eyes I saw the heads of two horses above me and our horse rearing up and refusing to go on, while Jim Joe's voice was shouting something at them.

I was on my feet in a flash. I remember we said nothing. It was one of those moments when the outcome didn't bear thinking about. All I remember is seeing our horse's feet above me. He wouldn't go any further. Jim Joe would have been sitting right at the back on the mowing machine seat and would have had his eyes on the ditch to his left, along which he would be trying to keep a straight line. The horses would have seen me long before he would. They stopped and that's what saved me.

Our horse, called Jim, was not a typical farm horse, being about one quarter race horse and inclined to shy away from anything unusual. He was young and lively, more lightly built for speed than heavy farm work and why my father bought him I don't know. He did enter him in a race, though, shortly after he'd bought him. The race was just a local affair in Coalisland, but, apparently, Jim threw the jockey off at the start and galloped off on his own. That was the end of his racing career, but he was a lovely animal and we were very fond of him.

Arthur, 16, with Jim the horse

One morning, my father put an empty sack on Jim's back, gave me a leg up and told me to take him to Coalisland to have him shod. I had only gone about half a mile when an evacuee from Belfast let fly at him with a catapult and hit him on the rump. Jim took off at a gallop and I only just managed to hang on. He stopped after about half a mile. No country boy would ever do such a thing, but this was a yobbo from the city who knew no better.

I arrived at the blacksmith's all right and brought my horse in. The blacksmith said he had to go into the town for a few minutes and asked me to wait. Well I waited and waited and it was an hour or more before he came back. I later found out that he was backing horses with a bookie as he had a gambling craze.

It was a cold day and the horse and myself were frozen. It was another hour or so before Jim was shod and ready. When we led him out I could tell he was on edge, cold and thirsty, as well. The blacksmith turned him round and gave me a leg up then he hit him with the flat of his hand. Well, that did it; Jim took off like a bullet. I threw myself down on his neck and held on with my knees and he broke into a gallop and there was no way to stop him – just cling on and hope we didn't meet anything. Lucky then there wasn't anything but bicycles on the road and they soon got out of the way, but, on rounding the next bend, I saw a car approaching. It belonged to the parish priest and he pulled up on the side of the hedge before I reached him. I was so glad he did.

When I was about halfway home, Jim stopped of his own accord and we were still in one piece. About a fortnight later on Sunday morning the parish priest was officiating at our church and decided to visit the local parishioners. When he arrived my mother introduced him to the family. When she said, "This is Arthur," he looked at me and said, "Are you the boy on the horse?" Then he lectured me about the dangers of riding so recklessly in the countryside. If he had only known that I had had the wits scared out of me and if I had hit that hard road I would have been lucky to be alive, but you didn't answer back in those days. You just said, "Yes, Father," and got away as quickly as possible.

Horse racing, or rather betting on the horses, was an interest to many in our area. The Lincolnshire Handicap and the Grand National were the first two big horse races of the year and were called the Spring Double. After that there was a big race about every month until the Manchester November Handicap which was the last. Big race fever would gradually build up among the punters. They no longer greeted you with, "Good morning," but rather, "Anything for the National?" or, "Anything for Saturday?" Papers were waited on around race days and were usually brought by the bread man. Two or three people would have it spread out on the wall at the corner while they read the tips. On Radio Eirann at ten o'clock each night there had to be dead silence while a ten minute programme was digested. This culminated in the selections for the next day and woe to anyone who coughed or scraped their chair.

As there were only two radios in the area, one of which was ours, people would call in at ten o'clock at night to hear the racing programme and get the tips, particularly before the big races, when the house would be packed. On the Sunday before the race, someone would be sent to Coalisland to get the *News of the World*. This was looked on as an immoral paper but it had tipped great winners in the past and one man used to take the racing page out and burn the remainder so that his family would not be contaminated.

The part that I enjoyed most was the discussions and arguments that took place in our house between Eileen's brother Jim Joe, Geordie Cullen, who came in most nights, and my father, who had his bibles and was trying to show them which was the form horse.

Geordie had a bet everyday, but usually his speculation amounted to sixpence. He would put sixpence on a horse, or maybe threepence each way, and the result onto another horse in the next race, and so on. Each day he would come in and tell us how nearly he had come to breaking the bookmaker. A short head had deprived his last horse when he was due to collect £5, but nobody believed him.

Dog racing, on the other hand, was more a hands-on occupation. My cousins on the next farm to the left of us kept greyhounds, which was a passion for John, who, like my father, had his greyhound bibles piled high. He could rattle off the lineage of a dog, both sire and dam, for generations back.

There was an official racing track in Dungannon, where John raced his dogs with moderate success. But then something happened that changed the whole racing scene, at least on a Sunday. A flapping track opened in Lurgan. This was an unlicensed track, unconnected to the Kennel Club, and all one had to do was bring your dog, call it what name you liked, and register it, colours and markings etc. Of course, you didn't give its real name, so form went out of the window. If I could get two and sixpence I would go on the train to Lurgan with the rest. The train would have come through Coalisland and Dungannon and the guard's van would be full of dogs.

Dogs would be getting a close scrutiny from the punters, looking for a clue as to their identity. We got to recognise most of the dogs after a time, but if a new one appeared he was carefully watched to see if he was being supported.

Then we had a coup. John had a fawn bitch which he raced occasionally, an average animal, but a man from Coalisland had another bitch almost identical which was a class animal called Madam Print. When they compared them they discovered that the only difference was that the good dog had a white tip on the end of its tail, almost two inches long.

John, James and Joe, the three brothers, experimented with colours and dyes and finally came up with the idea of dipping the tale in yellow distemper on Sunday morning. I was over there after Mass to see the operation performed and it looked perfect when it dried. The only danger was if the weather broke, as it was cloudy bright and James was put in charge to ensure that Madam Print was covered if rain threatened.

When the dogs went into the holding kennels, all was well and if it didn't rain in the race then we could all relax. I suppose I raised my usual 2/6d which left me with a two shilling bet after the train fare. Madam Print won easily at a good price under her new name, because there was another good ringer in the race as well. John's other dog wouldn't have had a chance in this company. The price drifted to 6-1, at which point I plunged with my two shillings. How rich I felt on my way home.

Another way to have a flutter was cock fighting. This was illegal in my time, but local people didn't take so much notice of the law in Derrytresk, especially as it was a very old hobby and had many adherents who took great pride in their prize birds. They were reared lovingly on only the best. If they were well looked after it was said they were well walked, and that meant they were well fed and on a dry, clean yard where they could take shelter, if necessary.

They were the aristocrats of the yard, and cock fanciers would stand for ages admiring them and discussing their finer points. And, yet, when they would take them off to the cock fights and lose, they would go home that night empty-handed. Their beautiful bird had been killed by another beautiful bird and it would be buried in some corner of a foreign field.

The venue would be kept very secret when a 'rumble in the jungle' was planned, usually for a holiday. If you had the intention of attending and you asked someone in the know, he would usually look over both shoulders before imparting the information.

I remember going once to a place called Sanseys Bottom. I knew where it was, but I had never been in there. When I got there and pushed my bike off the road, as instructed, I found I was in a puzzle of little roads and paths and bushes. There was dead silence and I knew that there would be about one hundred people in there some place. Then I heard a little cackle, then another and I was guided into a clearing of silent men getting cocks spurred up and ready to fight.

The birds' ordinary spurs had been sawed off with a hacksaw leaving only a stump. And on this the steel spurs were placed carefully by the handler, as one of these could give a deep wound in the hand. These spurs were about three or four inches long and curved to point forward right at the opponent's heart. Small pieces of chamois leather were wrapped around the stump until the ring of the steel spur fitted tightly. Then it was tied in place with pieces of waxed string called wax end. Afterwards, the handler would hold it up in front of him and look along it with great care to check the spur was in alignment.

When a pair had been weighed and matched, the betting would start and eventually the handlers would step into the ring and release the birds. Each time one of the birds was spurred by the other, a handler would lift it and separate them before the next round. It was a fight to the death, unless one ran away, which didn't happen very often, and meant that their breeding was at fault.

Those men whose birds lost the fight would toss their pride and joy under the hedge without a backward glance. One man came home from Ballenderry cock fights and his wife asked him how he got on.

"Lizzie, Lizzie," he said. "Your cock lies dead on Ballenderry shore." Very poetic.

Talking of fighting, we had a black and white collie type dog called Sport. He came from the same litter as Johnny Campbell's brown and white dog, Jack. Johnny owned the next farm but one to us and had to take his cows past our house to the Brilla bog each morning – and each morning Sport would be waiting for him. Jack would also be watching out for Sport and they would make as much noise as a dozen dogs barking and howling at each other through the railings.

Occasionally, a fight would take place and they were so well matched that they would go rolling over and over along the road while Johnny and I tried, at great risk, to get hold of them. Eventually, we would pull them apart and drag them away snarling at each other. No harm done, we could see.

One day I was going past Johnny's house with Sport, and Jack was waiting to pounce through a hole in the hedge. Johnny heard the row and came out to help. By this time they were locked together on the road. Each one had got a hold and neither would give way. I saw that Sport had got Jack by the neck and Jack had hold of Sport's foreleg in his mouth and neither would let go.

I realised that Jack could crunch Sport's forepaw with his powerful jaws any time he wished. As they weren't moving, I could see that he was just keeping enough pressure to hold him firm but not to break his leg. This wasn't a fight to the death at all. It was just another round of sound and fury.

Eventually we pulled them apart and I could almost hear them say, "Thanks very much and I'll see you tomorrow."

CHAPTER THIRTEEN

There were a few very witty people around our area. It seemed to run in families and did not depend on education or intelligence, as far as I could see. It was just a gift. There was a family of McCanns in Derryloughin, the next townland to Derrytresk, and the father Matt was the head wit, although his son Hughie was just as good. One or two of Matt's one liners I still hear even to this day being told in a modern version.

During the war in the 1940s all the men had jobs in the building trade, either at the new aerodrome in Ardbo or in Belfast. Matt worked in Belfast and was in digs with a few of his mates from Derryloughin. Needless to say, the food would not have been very good, owing to the rationing, and rabbit was the main meat dish at dinner, night after night.

Matt had dropped hints about the bunny diet, but all in vain. One night at dinner, after a rabbit stew, one of the men became ill with stomach cramps and vomiting. The landlady was getting very agitated and asked if he had been drinking on the way from work. He had had a drink and she decided that that was, of course, the cause of his sickness. She had thought they had better get the doctor.

Matt, who had been sitting puffing at his pipe after his dinner and saying nothing, as usual, broke his silence.

"Mrs. Conroy," he said. "That man doesn't need a doctor, he needs a ferret."

Matt's brother, Dan, was just as witty as Matt. A neighbour of Dan's got married to a nurse who was also a neighbour. They were both middle aged and refined and, perhaps, more well-read than the ordinary population of the area. Anyone who is different always attracts attention. If you are not one of the lads then you will be picked on, just like the school playground, again.

When Dan came into the shop one day for his quarter ounce of plug tobacco, my father asked him how his newly married neighbours were settling in.

"It's a great advantage to have a fully qualified nurse living with you," said Dan.

"Well, it would be indeed, if you were ill," said my father.

"I called in to see them yesterday," said Dan, "John had been digging down in the bottom field and he came in and nearly fell into his armchair. 'Whatever is the matter, dear?' said Susan going over and taking his pulse. 'I feel so worn out suddenly,' said John.

"Well, Susan went over to the sideboard, and lifted a little bottle of tablets. She took one out and went to the sink for a glass of water. 'Just take this, dear,' she said, 'and you will feel much better.'"

"Well," said Dan, "John sat for a few minutes after he'd taken the tablet then he tightened his cap on and off he went at the double down the field. He grabbed the spade and the sods started flying again. Oh, James, it would be marvellous to have somebody like that in the house with you."

No one would believe Dan's tales, but you were never sure.

Matt's son Hughie, who had inherited the spontaneity of wit, once again made John the butt of the joke. You see, John would not be found playing pitch and toss at the corner or in the pub for a Guinness.

Men's trousers at that time were very high waisted and were held by braces. If one happened to be a bit short bodied then, if they fitted properly, the top would reach almost chest high. This was John's problem and, to make matters worse, he pulled his braces so tightly that it almost seemed as if he had a hump. It gave the impression of great tension in the braces.

Sitting in Matt McCann's one night, which was a great ceilidhing house – ceilidh meaning 'visit' in English – the subject of John's braces came up for discussion. Hughie, who had been playing a selection of reels and jigs on his violin, at which he was an expert, paused when he heard the subject of the discussion. Somebody said it was just possible, the way John's shoulders were hunched, that he gave this impression of tension.

"Indeed not," said Hughie. "I was talking to him yesterday. Those braces are as tight as that E string on my fiddle. If I'd had a knife and cut those braces he would have shot out of those trousers and landed in the Blackwater River."

As I have mentioned, Matt's was a great place to ceilidh. One night during the 1940s Matt, who had been somewhere on his ceilidh, came home at eleven o'clock. It was a freezing cold night and when he walked in he saw all us young fellows sitting around the big turf fire. This was a wooden and zinc house built on the moss and it was not very warm. I remember Matt standing behind us just looking, then he turned and walked out. In a minute he returned and said, "God, Belfast is getting it tonight."

We rushed out, as Belfast was plainly visible at night on the other side of Lough Neagh, but all was quiet. We came in again and Matt was sitting on his favourite chair lighting up again.

"There are no bombs," we said.

"Ah, they must have stopped then," he said. He knew how to handle us.

Matt's Hughie was with us once when we had been listening to motorbike racing on the radio. Afterwards we were going home and someone started imitating the commentator saying things like, "Here comes Pat the Guy on a Norton," or, "Here comes Felix Wallace on a BSA," picking old men who could probably hardly walk. Each one was received with loud laughter and applause.

In Coalisland there was an oldish English lady called Miss Rogers who had a little sweet shop which we used to frequent. She sold minerals and buns when we called there for refreshments when we were young. She chatted away to us in her English accent – a nice old lady.

So we all had a go at thinking up the most ridiculous coupling for the motor race talk. Hughie waited until we were all finished and then he said, "Here comes Miss Rogers on a scallop." A scallop is an osier rod used for thatching, which bends without breaking. It is also used for making baskets. Well, the thought of Miss Rogers astride a scallop, like the wicked witch of the north, was too much for us and the laughter went on for a long time. Hughie had won again.

My cousin Joe and myself used to go shooting ducks and rabbits etc. on a regular basis. We had a flat-bottomed boat – I think it was called a cot – and one day we were down along the river looking for wildfowl, but there was nothing.

Then Joe had a brain wave. "Why not take the boat and row out to Scady Island in Lough Neagh," said Joe.

I was much younger than Joe and didn't appreciate the danger of a flat-bottomed boat in a storm and readily agreed. It was quite a long way from the Brilla; first, down the river to the lough, which was a few miles, then I don't know how far out to Scady Island. I'm not sure if it was visible. I only know that it seemed some distance from us. No matter how fast we rowed we didn't seem to get any nearer.

We patrolled the island keeping quiet and covered much of it, but not a duck in sight. We could see ducks flying past, all well out of range. So, after a rest, we decided to go back. No sooner were we in the boat than the wind started to blow and the next minute we were in a storm. We were heading straight into the wind to get back to Mahery, which was on the mouth of the river, but we were being blown back in our flat-bottomed boat and making no headway.

Joe was rowing and he said, "We can't make it to Mahery. We'll go with the wind to Roskeen Point," which we could see jutting out in the distance. Once we turned with the wind we began to make good speed. As the cot bounced up and down like a cork over the waves, Joe gave one of his big laughs and said, "I wouldn't like to be grabbing for the rushes now."

If he thought he was frightening me, he was right, but with the help of the gale behind us, we made Roskeen, tied up the boat, took our guns and walked all the way back. Next morning we walked back to get the boat and then rowed back again. What a catastrophe – all that and never got a shot.

I kept saying to Joe, "Who was the bright boy who said go to Scady Island?"

Lough Neagh was home to a freshwater trout called pullen. Fishermen's lads used come round with a bucket selling them and we didn't appreciate how lucky we were to have them, as they were delicious, and, as usual, familiarity breeds contempt. I wish I could get one now. There was a big eel fishing industry, as well. I remember being down at a house owned by a man called Johnny McIlkenny, down near the river one night having a drink or two, and about one o'clock in the morning he said to me, "Come down to the river and help me get some eels."

There was a path across the meadow to the river nearby and Johnny lifted a rope that was tied to a large wire tank in the river and pulled it into the bank. As he raised it up there seemed to be fifty to a hundred eels thrashing about. Johnny took one or two out, I forget how many, and we brought them to the house. I think maybe he had about half a dozen, as it was quite a party that night.

Johnny had a cement floor in the kitchen and he said, "Now, Arthur, I'll show you how to kill an eel." He killed the first one by lifting it out by the head, with thumb and fingers tightly holding, then throwing it hard against the cement floor and the eel was knocked unconscious. I managed to do it first time and was quite proud.

When Johnny and I were going out to get the eels, he had said to his wife, "Have that pan spitting hot, Cassie," and, sure enough, the pan was spitting. The eels were skinned and cooked and I don't think I've ever tasted anything so beautiful.

CHAPTER FOURTEEN

I f I wanted to know anything important I always asked Kathleen. She used to say, "Arthur and I are twins – we've got the same noses." So, after I left the Academy and was working on the farm, I gradually began to think that perhaps I should have taken a chance on being educated.

We were joined with Tom Gartland and we started the ploughing in springtime. This must have been the second year as I was home for two years altogether. Anyway, this particular day I went over to plough Tom's top field but I found that he had dug deep trenches down the field and, as it was clay soil and had been a very dry spring, the spadefuls of soil had just dried like bricks and adhered to each other.

Tom handed me a spade and told me to fill in the trenches. I tried all right, but it would have taken the rest of the spring to fill those trenches, and only then with the aid of a pickaxe. In the afternoon I stood there, thinking about farming, and I realised I wasn't as fond of it as before and I should have taken the chance of being educated when I had it.

The treatment by Tom had just tipped the balance so I consulted Kathleen, my mentor, and she consulted my father, and like the good man he was he let me go back to college. This was very good of him as we had to get a man in to replace me and my father was getting on a bit at the time.

I wouldn't go back to the Academy, though, because I knew I would never work enough to pass exams unless I was imprisoned in a boarding school, because I still hated school. So I told Kathleen I wanted to go to Armagh, where I couldn't get out and would have to study. She wrote off to Armagh for me and I was allowed to go.

So back I went and did my three years porridge and was ready for the next stage of my life.

Being at Armagh wasn't all bad. I loved Gaelic football and played it every day after class. I was lucky in that I was there the year Armagh won the All Ireland College's football at Croke Park. Players like Iggy Jones, Jim Devlin, Eddy Devlin, Gerry O'Neill from Armagh, Pat O'Neill from Keady, lads from Derry and Louth – I can't remember their names but all very good footballers.

Iggy Jones, the footballer

Iggy Jones was, of course, the one who impressed me most. When he got the ball he'd run toe to hand along the sideline for about twenty yards, stop suddenly, which would mean his marker would have to put the brakes on as well, then he would take off again, then he would stop suddenly again. This was stamina-sapping for whoever was marking. When he finally made the last burst he would cut in across the field and shoot over the bar.

When I left Armagh college, I started playing football for Derryloughin Kevin Barries. The team had only been formed a couple of years earlier and hadn't really got a permanent football pitch, but the lads were all keen and willing and that meant a lot. I had played a couple of games for Derrytresk previously, but I was persuaded by Matt's Paddy, our goalkeeper, to join Derryloughin and I thought there would be more craic there.

Paddy was Matt's eldest son and was a very funny man. The whole family were comedians, except they wrote their own stuff, as it were. We had a full back called James who was a good experienced back and didn't mind dishing out a bit of punishment to the opposing forwards if they presumed to take liberties with his person. James was known by the nickname 'Pocket Legs'. I think it was because his legs were slightly bowed but I don't know where it originated.

He was a sincere, innocent sort of fellow who would ask you, "How did I play?" and, "Was there many bragging me on the touchline?" He really lived for the game. I think over the years he was our best player. He took great pleasure in telling me how high up he jumped for the ball and what a catch he made.

One day we happened to be all together on the high bridge, myself, James and Matt's Paddy. I had a camera with me and we decided to take a picture of James jumping for the ball. Paddy threw the ball up in the air and I took the photograph. We had to wait to develop it, of course, and I brought the picture down to the clubhouse for James to see. Imagine his surprise when all that was on the photograph was James' legs hanging down from the top of the photograph, just above the knee. I'm afraid I had made a bloomer.

Then we showed it to Paddy and right away he came to the rescue.

"You've jumped too high, James. You've jumped out of the photograph."

That pleased James. "I jumped out of the photo," he announced proudly. "I jumped too high."

That black and white photograph of Pocket Legs' legs became well known in folklore after that. I think everyone in the district knew of Pocket Legs' legs.

The standard of football played in Tyrone and, indeed in Northern Ireland, was very low. All the good teams were down south and the championship was always won by teams like Kerry or Cavan. Compared to the Tyrone team of today we were not in the same league; we didn't have any Peter Canavans then, well, perhaps, one. I imagine the Tyrone team of the forties wouldn't have beaten a good club team in Kerry. But the "Barries" didn't mind and we all enjoyed ourselves.

At that time, toe to hand football as exemplified by Iggy Jones, was in its infancy. It improved the game immensely. Brocagh had a seven-a-side team which were very successful because they were all exponents of the art. Kevin Tague, Kevin Canavan, Peter O'Neill, Hairy Dan, as we called him – I think his name was also Canavan – and Joe Scullion, their full back, among others, made up the Brocagh team and they were great to watch.

Discipline was not very good and some teams preferred to fight instead of play football. One of these was the Windmill and there was sure to be a fight if you went there.

One Sunday we had to go to the Windmill and we knew for sure that a fight would start, so we took our curate, Father Murphy, with us as insurance. But they took no notice of the priest and started the fight early in the match. It was like little fires breaking out all over the pitch. I was standing, wondering about what was going on, when someone grabbed my arms from behind and another started to batter me on the face. Next thing Father Murphy ordered us all back to the bus, but getting through the gate was another matter.

In front of me I saw one of our footballers, Jimmy Taggart, being beaten over the head by a woman with an umbrella, and our chairman, James McAliskey, laying about him with a bicycle pump. But we managed to get to the coach, which was hit by a couple of bricks before we got away.

In my time we didn't win anything, but I enjoyed every minute of it. We kept the team alive for future teams to win honours, which they duly did. They also serve who only stand and wait.

The first day that I went to see Derrytresk, or the Hill, as it was called, play the team consisted of

James and Pat O'Neill (Ned's), Barney O'Neill (Fat) the three Campbells and two Fitzgeralds (Red boys), among others.

Like Derryloughin, very often the team would be short of players, so an unsuspecting man would be commandeered from the sideline, who just took off his jacket and maybe even played in a pair of boots. Ned O'Neill, the father of Pat and James, was a keen supporter but he kicked every ball himself as he watched from the sidelines – anyone who stood in front of him did so at their peril. Sometimes a chap called Colm Murray who came down from Dungannon at weekends to visit his aunt would be pressed into service. But Colm taught Irish dancing to the girls in Dungannon and he wasn't what one would call a robust character and consequently got many a blessing showered on him from Ned.

"Bad luck to Colm," he would say, as he aimed another kick at nothing.

One day they pressed into service Paddy McCann (Scotch), who had learned to play soccer on the streets of Glasgow. When Paddy got the ball he dropped it on the ground and tried to dribble it towards the goal, which is fine in soccer but certainly not Gaelic football. Old Ned nearly had a fit.

The team changed into their strip along the sideline beside a hedge and dressed afterward at the same spot. Not much privacy there. At half time they would congregate there for a smoke and sometimes a Woodbine would be shared between two or three. At that time smoking was really supposed to be good for you and a woodbine at half time would help the players' breathing.

My cousin Joe played midfield and I noticed that he had very long legs, not knowing that I had the same legs myself.

The team was called Derrytresk, Fir Na Cnuic, Gaelic for men of the hill. Recently the Derrytresk team got into a national final and would probably have won it only the game ended in a fight. Nothing has changed.

One Sunday, a few years after I had left Armagh College, Derryloughin had to play Dungannon in the cup in Coalisland. We had no preparations or plans to deal with the phenomenon that was Iggy Jones and when I saw him appear on the field and take over his right three-quarter spot, I looked around to see who was marking him. There was nobody so I had to mark him myself.

Well, he immediately started his caper of streaking up the sideline with me keeping just inside him. Then he'd stop dead, then away he sprinted again, but when he got to the other end I was still there and he had to centre the ball, and that's how it went all through the first half.

In the second half it was the same again. Only once did he get close enough to shoot. I was in front of him with my hands held high – he put a drop shot between my legs and Joe Donnelly made a great save.

The final whistle went, but he never scored. That night I couldn't sleep a wink. I had called on such reserves of stamina that it took a long time for me to recover.

Incidentally, we lost the game – someone else did the scoring. I was so engrossed in my private battle with Jones that I had no idea what the score was. I wonder if one had a choice between Peter Canavan and Iggy Jones, who would play?

As the song says, "Those were the days my friend, we thought they'd never end." But they do.

CHAPTER FIFTEEN

When I passed all my exams and left Armagh College aged nineteen I still had no idea what I was going to do with my life. I ended up becoming a pharmacist, simply because a friend of Kathleen's who was working as a pharmacist in Portadown, told her about an apprenticeship that was going in one of the chemists there and suggested I apply for the position.

So I served my apprenticeship in McAnallen's in Thomas Street. This had a good dispensary business but as it had a lady proprietor it specialised in cosmetics and, being a farmer's son, I would have been much better in a chemist specialising in the veterinary business. I was very interested in cattle and horses and well used to them but, at the time, that was all that was available and I sort of drifted into it.

We were next door to the Queen's Hotel and we had a storeroom/workroom on its top floor. At that time the pharmacist made everything up from scratch, not like today, when it's just packets of tablets. Everything was made on the premises and sometimes it could take some time to do, so usually customers were asked to call back for their prescriptions. However, if it was something easy I would tell the customer to wait for a minute and hand it out to him. But most customers would call back and, if they couldn't, we would deliver the prescriptions, which were wrapped in white paper and sealed with sealing wax.

There were a few chemists in Portadown. Pedlow's in the Square, Davy Row on Woodhouse Street, Hendron's on West Street and another opposite Marley's in the Square was called, I think, the Medical Hall, where there was a bevy of glamorous girls working.

In the mornings we would visit Thoms café just across the road for a coffee and a doughnut. Also across the street from us was a record shop where they played all the latest hits. I can remember one day listening to Howard Keel singing "The girl that I marry" like it was yesterday. Next door to us was a music shop where I used buy strings for my banjo mandolin.

Arthur, 19, sitting on the hedge in front of the house, playing the banjo.

During the war we made our own leg tan, as nylons were no longer available. Our leg tan was very popular and I would go up to the room above the Queen's and spend an afternoon making the leg tan and bottling it.

We had a very good formula, because it didn't streak, it stayed on and it didn't soil clothing. Golden brown was our most popular shade. Customers used to call some products and colours by the queerest of names in different places I worked. In one shop a hair colour we sold was called Belle Colour, and I was asked for a bottle of Belly Colour. Probably the best one was when a lady came in and asked for a colour called Golden Squint and when I looked I found it was Gold Sequins. Another lady asked for a bottle of Helter Skelters meaning Alka Seltzer and, on one occasion, a man asked me for something for his wife's cystitis. I made him up a bottle of potassium citrate mixture. I put the direction on it which, at that time, was all written by hand and at the bottom of the label I wrote Mist Pot Cit which was shorthand Latin and purely for my own benefit lest he wanted a repeat. A short time later he returned and said I had given him the wrong bottle because it was for a Miss Pat Cit. It did look a bit like that but I have never heard of anybody yet called Cit.

After I qualified as a pharmacist, I worked in Belfast in the summer doing locums. A friend from Tyrone called Brendan Fee was also working in a chemist in the city and, as we both liked a bet, we would go down to the dog races at Dunmore Park on Thursday evenings.

We never won much, I remember, but if we lost we probably thought that the entertainment made it worthwhile. We would study the card and weigh up form and talk to somebody who knew somebody who knew somebody who knew the owner or trainer, but we never showed much profit.

One night Brendan was studying the card when he said, "Well, look who's here. It's my old friend, we'll have to go and see him."

Then he explained how he came to meet an oldish chap who owned a dog called 'On the Level'. "He will be over near the kennels," he said, and sure enough, there he was sitting by himself on a wall.

Brendan had explained to me that this man had, at first, trained the dog himself without success and, finally, he had given it to a trainer to have it done professionally. His pet name for the dog was Darkie and, having left him with the trainer for about a month, he had a call asking him to come down to see the dog having his first race. When he arrived he told Brendan he was shocked to find his little fat dog was now, what he called, skin and bones and his first words were, "That's not my wee Darkie."

"Oh, indeed it is," said the trainer. "And, I'm hoping you'll see an improvement tonight and, if you're a betting man, keep it small."

So, Darkie, or On the Level, as his racing name was, turned out to be a pretty useful dog, not breaking records but just useful. His one great asset was that he was out of the traps first every time and that meant he was never troubled on the first bend, where the hare would suddenly go to the left and this could bring a pile-up as the outside dogs would cut across the others. This happened quite often, but On the Level benefitted another two lengths when it did.

On the night in question, Brendan introduced me. We had a nice chat and he told us that the trainer said he had a chance, but a dog from Dungannon called Cool Kill was running and he was going to be hot favourite so be careful. Then we heard that another dog had come from Dublin who was also fancied, so poor Darkie's chances became slimmer, as was reflected in the betting, as Cool Kill and Palm Beach opened at even money, and On the Level drifted to 9-1. It was obvious what the bookies thought about it.

Well, I had a bet on it at 9-1 and Brendan thought I was a fool. The race started and On the Level was out in a flash with a two length lead going up to the first bend. The two favourites, who were slowly away, were eating up the lead ominously. At the bend they were only a length behind when the outside dog suddenly cut across them causing a terrible scramble and crowding them all onto the rails.

On the Level had now three lengths lead and the two favourites were after him neck and neck on the straight. They were catching up the lead so fast that it looked only a matter of time. As they came to the top bend they were nose to tail and both were passing him on the outside when the outer of them, who had his head just in front, tried to cut across and baulked the inside dog and they lost another length.

On the Level, which was on the rails, was heading for the line on the back straight but the other two dogs were closing rapidly again. They were at his shoulder with a couple of lengths to go, but he had his head in front as he crossed the line. Brendan and I went for a celebratory pint.

We used to go upstairs to watch the races so that we could stand and look down on the finishing line. If there was a photo finish we could see the winner if we were directly over the line, even if it was just a head in front. One night a fawn dog and a black dog were in a photo finish. The fawn dog won by a head, I could plainly see. Brendan said the fawn dog and I agreed. The bookies were shouting 4-1 the black dog and 1-8 the fawn one. I said to Brendan, "We know the fawn dog has won. Why don't we go down and collect a pound for nothing? That's a good bet for the next race."

"No, I won't."

"Well," I said, "I either believe my eyes or I don't, so I'm going down." And I went and found I had £16 and the bookie said, "£2 to £16," gave me a ticket, and the next minute I handed it back and collected £18. If that wasn't a certainty, surely nothing was.

I will never forget that fine sunny day
The day of the sports at the Washing Bay
The sun was shining on the water so blue
And the pipe band was playing O'Donnell a Bu
The water lay warm on the smooth silken sand
As we splashed and caroused
to the strains of the band
Then we had ice cream and minerals and buns
And lay on the warm grass to dry in the sun
At one we ran in the three legged race
Until we tripped up and I fell on my face
So we ran in the sack race until you broke your lace
And then you came third in the egg and spoon race
When the cycle race finished we went over the field
And watched our big sister dancing a reel
Then Granuaille's wife came looking for pennies
Singing her song but we didn't give any
But slipped away to where the high jump was on
And sat on two chairs as their owners had gone
It was there that I think we both closed our eyes
For when we woke up we got a surprise
Lots of people were going so it must have been late
So we both jumped up and we ran for the gate
Mammy stood there looking around
We ran up to her and fell on the ground
"We thought you had gone and got such a fright."
She put her arms round us and just held us tight.
I'll never forget that beautiful day
We went to the sports on the banks of Lough Neagh

CHAPTER SIXTEEN

We had an inland holiday resort, or it could have been, called The Washing Bay, about two miles from our house. It was just a little bay on the lough shore. The ground around it was a mixture of sand and peat, soft and dry in the summer months, and the lake had a smooth sandy bottom, which was ideal for children to play in as it was only one foot deep for about fifty yards and then it would get gradually deeper. The water in it was like a warm bath when the sun shone and the little kids revelled in it.

Sports meetings were held by the parish each year and there was a cinder bicycle track for racing, as well. When I was about twenty the parish gave up having the sports meetings, so our football club, the Derryloughin Kevin Barries, took over. As secretary I had the job, with the help of my very able committee, of running the sports meeting.

That was quite an experience the first time and I would have been completely lost, except for a few very experienced men. For example, the first race was the 100 yards sprint and I was surprised to see the turnout from the towns, such as Dungannon Harriers, all in their whites and looking very professional.

I had an old boy from the Academy helping me to organise it. He was a high jumper called Jack Quinn from Stewartstown. I didn't know he would be there, but we had been together at the Academy and he gave me instructions and advice.

He said, "When we hold the tape at the finish of the 100 yard sprint, don't bother trying to see who's won. Just look at me and when they break the tape and I point to the man that wins it, you point, too."

How lucky I was to have Jack, as three or four men broke the tape together and I wouldn't have had a clue. Jack walked over to the winner and I followed. He knew their names and, I suppose, he got it right. There was no protest.

It wasn't such a good day, weather wise, but the club made a small profit after prizes had been paid for.

On the Sunday morning of the Washing Bay Sports I went down early to measure the course for the races. Everything was simple enough until I started measuring the circular track for the bicycle races.

I don't know now how long the course was but I had a long tape which I pinned to the ground then walked along letting it out to its full length, then giving it a sharp pull and the spring brought it back to me. I repeated the process until I reached my marker again but instead of keeping a note of the number of tape lengths, I carried it in my head and in the end I wasn't sure what the number was. I don't remember now what the exact figures were but let's say it was either twenty or twenty-one tape lengths and if each tape was twenty yards that would mean that over twenty laps, the course could be about 400 yards short.

I looked at my watch and I hadn't much time, so I took the shorter length as I was more convinced that was right. During one of the cycling races it was announced that this race was for the Ulster Championship and as the cyclists were all flying around the track, I was away attending to something else, although I was listening to the commentary on the loud speaker. I heard the commentator say, "This track is very fast today and records could be broken." I felt sick but eventually the race finished and no record was broken. Thank goodness for that, I thought.

We had a mile race confined to the parish and our local lads were a bit shy, and in spite of much persuasion refused to take part. But someone had to race so I and two others from the football team did start the race. One dropped out and I ran on with the other lad who was left. We were jogging around and chatting but when we came to the final bend he took off like a greyhound and was about ten yards away before I got after him. I overhauled him but when I went to pass him he dug his elbows into my ribs a couple of times and I was going so flat out that I was unable to move away sideways. So I tried again to pass him and out came the elbow again. As we crossed the line I was about six inches in front. I couldn't believe it but it didn't matter as there were no prizes.

At that time there was a great runner from County Cork who was in the news called John Joe Barrie. He was making a big name for himself in running and was nicknamed the Ballanacurrie Hare. Our sports' dance was held in the evening after the sports in the

Brocagh AOH hall. When I arrived at the hall there were two chaps standing near the ticket collector and I overheard one of them remark, "There goes the Ballanacurrie Hare." Fame at last!

CHAPTER SEVENTEEN

When Kathleen qualified as a nurse and midwife she went to a job in Glasgow which she found, on arrival, was in a slum area of that city and from what she told me it resembled the recent programme on the BBC, *Call the Midwife*.

The police and everybody were very protective to the nurses, as the area was not very salubrious or safe to travel around, especially in the dark winter evenings.

One night she was called out to a tenement flat. The patient was a young black woman who gave birth to twins – two boys.

She said to Kathleen, "Will you choose names for them?"

Kathleen replied, "Peter and Arthur," after her boyfriend and her brother.

Kathleen only stayed in Glasgow for about a year and then went to Roe Valley hospital in County Fermanagh which was as complete a contrast as one could get.

I often wondered what became of little Peter and Arthur.

Peter, Kathleen's boyfriend, emigrated to America. On the Sunday night before he sailed we were all in Mahery, as usual, at the dance. Near the end the band played the waltz, "Now is the hour for me to say goodbye, Soon I'll be sailing far across the sea", which was a hit tune at the time and was made famous by film star Gracie Fields. After that, Kathleen would be in tears when she heard that tune. Kathleen took over the shop after that for two years or maybe more, until one day Peter returned and all was well.

They were married and settled down as proprietors of a central hotel in County Meath. It was in the middle of the farming area and, apart from market day, trade was slow during the day. Like farmers everywhere, when they have finished their milking and feeding their cattle and pigs, they are usually ready to go out for a pint about ten o'clock, so from then on trade would be brisk.

Once, when Shamey and I were staying there for a day or two, we were upstairs in their private lounge with Kathleen, when Peter called up, "Arthur, Shamey, come down." He was trying to put a man out who was causing trouble in the bar – a big hefty man who wouldn't budge and Peter was shoving him through the door where the man had wedged himself.

Shamey, Peter and I managed to push him through the doors and close them, then opened the big outer doors and shoved him out onto the street.

When we went up to Kathleen she asked who was it and when I told her she said, "Oh, glory be, he's a justice of the peace." I could hardly believe my ears and then she added, "And we are appearing before him next week."

I asked what for and she said, "For serving drinks after hours."

We were leaving the next day, but she told me he came in the following day very contrite, had a brandy and apologised. I believe when her case came up, it was dismissed.

Arthur (around 1990) in the Brilla
Photo shows the Brilla in County Tyrone on the left, the Blackwater River, and County Armagh on the right.

Like Kathleen, I also moved 'abroad' and arrived in England in 1954. I got off the boat in Liverpool at about seven o'clock in the morning and looked around for a café or restaurant to have some breakfast. I saw a policeman and crossed over the road and asked him about the nearest café.

He put his arm around me, "Ah, Paddy, how are you? Come with me and I'll take you to a good breakfast." And off we went with his arm still around me. He was really pleased to see me and I found out soon enough that, at that particular time, to be Irish would have opened doors in England. If you were Irish then you were going to be full of fun, make everyone laugh and, probably, sing a song, as well.

Arthur, standing, with his cousin Joe Magennis, whose father, Joe, emigrated to America.

Unlike Kathleen, I didn't move back to Ireland but stayed in England and made my life here...but that's another story. Maybe, I'll tell it to you later.

End